Final Destination 2

Howard Mahmood

FADE IN:
INT. DARK ROOM - NIGHT
TITLES OVER:
A padded wall is papered with NEWSPAPER CLIPPINGS that date back to the early 1900s:
"LOCAL FOWLER BROTHERS LOSE $35 TICKETS TO BOARD TITANIC" appears over "FOWLER BROTHERS KILLED IN COAL MINE MISHAP." Another series of articles reads, "JEWISH PROFESSOR DENIED ADMITTANCE TO HINDENBURG" and "PROFESSOR RABINOWITZ KILLED IN AVALANCHE." Etc...
Continuing along the wall, the newspaper articles all focus on the fates of the original SURVIVORS of the FLIGHT 180 CRASH.
We DISSOLVE between the various headlines depicting the gruesome deaths of Tod, Terry, Ms. Lewton, Billy Hitchcock, Carter and Alex
Browning.
Also in the mix are various CRIME SCENE PHOTOS of the deaths.
Decapitated torsos, crushed, mangled bodies, the charred remains of another and the face- down body of Alex Browning.
MAPS line the walls as well, pinpointing the locations of numerous deaths, perhaps seeking a pattern. Charts that timeline bizarre deaths, seating charts of downed aircraft, etc...
LATEX -GLOVED HANDS tear out the last article, apply fun- tack to its corners and place it in the center of all the others:

A REMEMBRANCE FOR THE VICTIMS OF FLIGHT 180
Friday marks one year anniversary.

END TITLES.
FLASH TO BLACK as a HAND ENTERS FRAME, PULL BACK TO REVEAL:

EXT. KIMBERLY'S NEIGHBORHOOD - DAY
KIMBERLY BURROUGHS, 19, puts a folded AAA map in her mouth. She opens the back of a RED NISSAN SUV, and pla ces her duffel bag inside.
That done, she lets the map drop from her mouth, catches it in her free hand and turns to hug her father, MR. BURROUGHS.

KIMBERLY
Thanks, Dad. I'll call you.

MR. BU RROUGHS
You have everything, Kimberly?
Credit card, cell phone, AAA card?

KIMBERLY
Relax, Dad. It's Daytona, not
Mongolia.

MR. BURROUGHS
(playful)
Fix -A-flat? Road flares?
Sunblock? Mace?

SHAINA (O.S.)
Condoms, handcuffs, lube?
Kimberly and Mr. Burroughs turn to see
SHAINA, 19, tall leggy brunette. Tan, tight tube top revealing her pierced navel,
Kimberly's best friend. She walks up the driveway with her bags.

SHAINA
Just kidding, Mr. B. Don't worry,
I'll keep an eye on her.

MR. BURROUGHS
(sarcastic)
Oh, that makes me feel a lot better.
Shaina throws her bags in, shuts the back and climbs in the SUV.
Kimberly hugs her dad, kissing him on the cheek.

KIMBERLY
I know this is the first time we've been apart since. But everything's gonna be okay.

MR. BURROUGHS
I know, honey. I just
Kimberly hugs him tighter. Cutting him off.

MR. BURROUGHS
Your mother would have been so proud of the way you've handled yourself through all
of this...

KIMBERLY
(softly)
I know, Dad.

SHAINA (O.S.)
Hello, the guys are waiting!
Kimberly gives him a quick kiss, jumps behind the wheel, starts the car and pulls away
as Shaina cranks up the sterco.

MR. BURROUGHS
Buckle up!
Mr. Burroughs waves as the girls roar off. As he looks down he spots an OIL STAIN
left by Kimberly's SUV. As he drags his shoe across the stain, a SLIGHT BREEZE
blows past his face.

CAMERA PUSHES IN as a look of concern crosses his face.

EXT. HIGHWAY ON RAMP - DAY
ON OLD WOMAN
As she pushes her supermarket cart up the on ramp. A SQUEAKY WHEEL is shrill
and disturbing.
DRIVERS of several waiting vehicles avoid staring at her weathered face as she passes.
Up ahead waiting in line, is Kimberly's red SUV.

UP AHEAD
Waiting in line, is Kimberly's red SUV.

SHAINA (O.S.)
Watch it!
Kimberly accidentally KISSES the bumper in front of her while daydreaming. She calls
out to the driver in front:

KIMBERLY
Sorry! My fault!
Shaina looks over, concerned. In the backseat, the guys DANO and
FRANKIE laugh hard and some of Frankie's milkshake comes out of his nose.

SHAINA
Want me to drive?

KIMBERLY
No, I'm good.
Shaina looks at Kimberly as a HAND suddenly hits Kimberly's window.
Kimberly spins around, startled.
Kimberly stares transfixed at the Old Woman, who stares back with chilling intensity.
The kids ad-lib "Let's go" and "Fucking freak." The Old Woman's
PLASTIC BAG BREAKS, sending oranges rolling down the on- ramp. The Old
Woman breaks eye contact with Kimberly as she rushes to retrieve them.
The signal turns from red to flashing yellow.
Kimberly pulls the SU V onto the highway, looking in the side view mirror to see the
Old Woman look up at her in SLOW-MO.

FRANKIE
Dano, shouldn't we go back and help your mother?

DANO
Blo w me.

CU ON KIMBERLY
As she looks back from the mirror and reacts to an ominous electronic road sign that
flashes "WARNING: CONSTRUCTION NEXT 180 FEET".

NISSAN SUV
Kimberly merging into traffic, NEARLY COLLIDES with a speeding yellow mini- bus carrying a high- school football team.
Kimberly nervously jerks the wheel to the right, then realizing she's speeding towards the road construction barrels, she swerves back left, right behind the mini-bus at the last moment.

CLOSE.
Kimberly pulls around the mini-bus as rowdy football players tackle each other, yelling:

FOOTBALL PLAYERS
Pile up! Pile up! Pile up!
Kimberly flicks on the radio and we hear HIGHWAY TO HELL by AC/DC at earsplitting volume. Kimberly and Shaina jump from the shock and reach to lower the volume.
Kimberly, disturbed by this, hits SEEK an oldies station. A GRISLY
CAR CRASH from Nervous Norvus' TRANSFUSION album.

DANO
Christ, is this tribute to Princess
Di Day or what?
Kimberly passes a car WEAVING on her right. The driver reaching into the back seat to quiet a BARKING DOG hanging on its head out the window.

KIMBERLY
(unnerved)
Jesus, all the crazies are out today.
A CLOUD passes Kimberly's head. She smells it and turns around, taking her eyes off the road to see Dano smoking a joint.

KIMBERLY
I told you no drugs in the car! My dad will freak!
Dano and Frankie exchange looks, God, what a geek!

DANO
(laughs)
Calm down, Kimmy. It's not drugs, just weed.

FRANKIE
Yeah, you should have specified.
Kimberly turns to Shaina, helpless. Shaina spins around, her eyes wordlessly tell Dano, I know she's a priss, but put it out.
Then Kimberly's CELL PHONE RINGS. She hits the speaker button.

MR. BURROUGHS (V.O.)

Kimberly? It's Dad.

KIMBERLY
Hey, Dad. What's up?
Dano defiantly blows more smoke toward Kimberly, then breaks into an unexpected coughing fit - looking over to see a HELLS ANGEL laughing at hi m. The biker's trashy GIRLFRIEND, also laughing, quickly FLASHES
HER TITS at Dano over:

MR. BURROUGHS (V.O.)
Your car's leaking either transmission or brake fluid. I want you to have it checked ASAP at a gas station.

KIMBERLY
You got it, Dad. I'll call you if
I have a problem.

MR. BURROUGHS (V.O.)
I mean it. Take care of it.

KIMBERLY
I will, Dad. Bye, luv you.
Kimberly passes a STATION WAGON on her right, the DRIVER squinting at a map while driving. A mattress and some furniture tied to the top
SHIFT as the wagon hits a bump.

SHAINA
Um, Kimberly, your dad's not gonna call like every ten minutes is he?
Before Kimberly can answer, Dano sees a CHP speeding up behind him.
He lowers the joint at once.

DANO
(hiding bag of weed in pants)
Shit! There's a cop behind us.
Pull into the right lane now!
Kimberly, scared, does as she's told nearly colliding with a speeding flat bed semi hauling a huge load of logs !
A HORN BLASTS. The truck swerves. Then speeds by on the right. A
COILED CHAIN drops down to the highway.

DANO
Look first, idiot!
Shaina turns up the radio and leans over to Kimberly.

SHAINA
Ignore 'em.

ON LOG TRUCK
One end of the RUSTY CHAIN holding the logs in place rattles on the pavement, sparking.
Looking in her rearview mirror, Kimberly turns pale - the COP pulls in behind her.

KIMBERLY
Dano, put that out NOW.
Dano takes one last drag and flicks the joint out the window. It bounces on the windshield of a FORD EXPEDITION to their left.

INSIDE THE EXPEDITION
KAT, 28, very corporate America, wears a navy blue power suit and speaks into a phone headset while smoking a cigarette.

KAT
No, I'm stuck on Jury Duty so I won't be able to pitch the campaign. Let's get Silverstein to come in and...
Kat sees the joint that smoulders in the dried leaves beneath her windshield wipers. A moment later, a small FLAME crackles.

KAT
What the hell? No, not you.
Kat flicks on her WINDSHIELD WIPER FLUID, successfully putting out the joint, but her worn wipers smear ash and fluid around, impairing her vision.
Kat turns and looks at
DANO, dead serious all of a sudden. Staring straight ahead.

DANO
What's the cop doing? Did he see that?
Kat sees the tailgating CHP, smiles, then resumes her conversation.

KAT
Forget it, I'll call him myself.
Kat hangs up, then looks down at her cell phone, squints and dials a number...

PAN OFF KAT TO OFFICER THOMAS BURKE
Early 20's, rookie cop, who seems to have missed the entire exchange.

INSIDE TIIE POLICE CAR
Thomas speaks into his radio.

THOMAS
I was supposed to be off today.
How did I get screwed?

DISPATCHER (O.S.)
No biggie. Drake called in sick.

THOMAS
Copy that.
(switches off; annoyed)
Go on, sleep it off Drake.
Thomas tries to sip from a McDonald's coffee cup on the dashboard, but it's TOO HOT.
He places it back on the dash.
The VIBRATIONS of the road make the COFFEE CUP slide closer and closer to the
edge of the dashboard.

BACK TO KIMBERLY'S SUV
Dano nervously looks back.

FRANKIE
Relax, dude.
But Kimberly still looks uneasy as her dashboard "Check Engine" light begins
flickering.
Kimberly spots a road sign Next Service 18 Miles.

KIMBERLY
This trip better be wor th it.
What's the guy- girl ratio again?

SHAINA
Get ready to smile, five guys per girl.

KIMBERLY
I can live with thaaaa
Kimberly stops mid-sentence when the WHITE VAN in front of her suddenly SLAMS
ON ITS BRAKES and pulls onto the shoulder for no reason. Kimberly SCREAMS,
swerving around the van just in time to avoid an accident. Frankie instinctively
SHOUTS at the van.

FRANKIE
What's your problem, ya fuckin' crack baby?!

INSIDE THE WHITE VAN
ISABELLA CRUZ, late 20's and VERY PREGNANT, drives a delivery van full of
funeral wreaths, crosses and classic rose urns. Most are marked: In Memory of Flight
180.
She chokes back sobs into a cell phone as she pulls over.

ISABELLA

...couldn't Keep your dick in check for another month? I knew this would happen when I got pregnant.
She pounds the steering wheel, furious.

ISABELLA
What'd the doctor say? I have to come in to test for STDs? Goddamn you, Jorge.
A CRATE in the back of her van topples over and CRASHES and a flurry of sunflower petals sails out the window. Isabella jumps in surprise and, wiping tears from her eyes, rolls up the windows as petals shower the visor of
EUGENE, the Harley Rider, who smears the petals (and some squashed bugs) around his visor and drops back.

INSIDE NISSAN SUV
Kimberly falls back into the right lane and looks uneasy as she sees a TRUCK DRIVER guzzling from a flask as it passes the SUV, revealing its side is an ad for FIRESTONE TIRES.
It finally clears frame, revealing a highway billboard that reads,

"DRUNK DRIVING KILLS."
Kimberly reaches back and pulls on her seatbelt in spite of laughter from the back seat.
Up ahead, the RUSTY CHAIN seems to have more give to it. LOGS STRAIN against it.
Suddenly, a black cloud of exhaust from a blue '83 Chevette in front of them causes everyone to roll up their windows.
OIL DRIPS from its rusty exhaust pipe. The thick exhaust BLINDS
Kimberly.

FRANKIE
Gas it around these idiots. We do have 1200 miles to go, you know.
Kimberly tires to enter the passing lane, but she's blocked by a
SUBURU WAGON. In the front seat, a seven- year old kid is sadistically
SMASHING two toy cars together.
Kimberly passes the Suburu and pulls up to a PACER. The Harley roars by, startling her.

INSIDE PACER
NORA KESNER, 35, and her son TIM, 15. Tim drums on the dashboard with two ten-ounce Naya bottles.

NORA
Tim, will you cut that out? I can't even hear myself think.
Tim frowns and then winces, holding his jaw.

TIM
Damn, it really hurts, Mom.

NORA
I know, we'll be there soon.
Tim drops the Naya bottles on the seat. One of them quietly falls to the floor, rolls a bit, finally settling UNDER THE BRAKE PEDAL.

INSIDE NISSAN SUV
Kimberly is still behind the smoke-spewing Chevette. She passes it on the left. Frankie rolls down his window.

FRANKIE
(yells to driver)
Ever hear of the Ozone layer, asshole?

INSIDE CHEVETTE
RORY, 27, leans down to snort a line of coke off a Def Leppard CD case. S he looks up to see the Patrol Car is now behind him, he reflexively taps the brakes.
Rory, eyes like saucers, sits rigidly transfixed at the wheel and nonchalantly wipes the CD clean on his pants.

INSIDE NISSAN SUV
She has dropped back behind the Chevette and CHP car and is running down along side of a BLACK TRANS AM.
Up ahead she sees the Hig hway Patrol Car flick on its LIGHTS and pull into the shoulder around the Chevette and behind the Semi loaded with logs.

INSIDE THE COP CAR
As Thomas pulls in behind the log truck, his coffee cup lurches forward, spilling hot coffee all over his lap and the floor.

THOMAS
Son of a bitch.

INSIDE TRANS AM
Its driver, EVAN SCHAEFFER, 21, flashes a cocky smile at Kimberly, clearly making Frankie jealous.

FRANKIE
A Trans Am. That shit went out with New Kids on the Block.

DANO
Yeah. Who does he think he is?
Knight Rider?

FRANKIE
(laughs; then)
Who?

Frankie leans out and tosses milkshake on Evan's window.

DANO
You know, Hasselhoff before he did
Baywatch.
Evan, pissed off, flips off Frankie. The windshield wipers smear around the thick milky fluid. The sun blinding him.

KIMBERLY
What's the chance of finding a nice mature guy once we get to Daytona?

SHAINA
How does a nice mature fuck sound?
Kimberly laughs, then leans in close to Shaina.

KIMBERLY
Hey, thanks for talking me into this trip. Ever since my mom... I dunno, I just feel like I'm starting to live again, you know?
Shaina smiles in understanding.

INSIDE POLICE CRUISER
Thomas bends to wipe up the mess. He only glances at the road as he tries to soak up the coffee.
Suddenly up ahead, THE RUSTY CHAIN SNAPS! The logs roll off the side of the truck onto the highway.
One bounces as it hits, and slams through Thomas' front winshield and out the back, taking Thomas' head with it.
EUGENE slams on his brakes. His Harley slides out and he is SLAMMED to the ground, sliding at 60 miles per hour across the highway, right in front of the yellow mini-bus.
The MINI- BUS DRIVER brakes to avoid Eugene. The FOOTBALL PLAYERS tumble forward and hit him in the head. He loses control and slides off the road onto the grass median.
He blows a front tire and the mini-bus begins to flip, ROLLING several times int o the oncoming lanes of traffic, and is HIT by a

MACK TRUCK.
Eugene slides into a huge log, and hits it with a sickening crunch.
Only to be HIT and CRUSHED by his sliding motorcycle.
Rory looks up too late and REAR ENDS Thomas' car, EXPLODING the gas tank and HURLING Rory's dead body halfway through the windshield where it remains half in/half onto the hood.
KAT, dialing, looks up, slams on her brakes, but SKIDS on oil from the Chevette.
She swerves into Kimberly, SIDE SWIPES her, then swerves to miss a huge log only to run head on into two more, flipping the
Expedition end over end right next to Kimberly.

Kimberly swerves back from being hit by Kat, just in time to see a huge log ahead. She tries to turn hard to the right to avoid it, but hits it broadside
Sending the SUV FLIPPING OVER the top of the log and SLIDING down the road.
Inside, Shaina, Dano and Frankie are tossed around like rag dolls, shredded by glass and shrapnel Frankie is EJECTED out the side window.
Kimberly's SUV slides to a stop on its side. She looks back to her mangled but still alive friends and up in time to see

NORA'S PACER
Nora sees the collisions ahead and slams on the brakes but the fallen
Naya bottle prevents her from braking, and she SLAMS into the back of
Kat's Expedition.
The crash test dummy collision folds her Pacer and it EXPLODES into a huge fireball.
EVAN, blinded by the smeared windshield, is too late. He swerves his
Trans Am around the burning cars onto the wet grass.
Kimberly sees the topless Trans Am slowly roll out of a huge WALL OF
FIRE and coast to a stop. Evan comes up battered and bloody but still alive. He is trapped in his burning car, screaming and trying to release the seatbelt.
Then, just when she thought it was over, a HUGE SEMI slides thro ugh the wall of fire, SMASHING the Trans Am out of the way, SPINNING it like a top. With the back sliding at 90 degrees it keeps on coming.

KIMBERLY'S POV
The semi's grill comes right at her!

CU ON KIMBERLY
She screams and we

CUT TO:
THE HIGHWAY O N RAMP - NISSAN SUV - 8 MINUTES EARLIER
Sweating profusely, Kimberly's eyes dart around, taking in her surroundings...

DANO (O.S.)
Flight 180. You know, that plane crash with those kids from Mount
Abraham.
The Old Woman BUMPS the window - scaring the shit out of everyone.
The kids ad-lib "Let's go" and "Fucking Freak!"
Kimberly stares in horror as the Old Woman flashes an evil grin.
Kimberly's eyes lower to the bag of oranges
Which BREAKS, exactly like before, and the Old Woman scurries after them. The signal turns from red to flashing yellow.

FRANKIE
Dano, shouldn't we stop and help your mother?

DANO

Blow me. Yellow means go,
Kimberly.
Kimberly hyperventilates in the driver's seat. Freaking. A yellow mini- bus with football
players speeds past.

KIMBERLY
Oh my god, oh my god...
Dano, confused, rolls a joint.

SHAINA
What is it? What are you?

KIMBERLY
There's going to be a huge accident! Everyone's gonna die.
All of us! I saw it!
Dano hums the Twilight Zone theme.

FRANKIE
That's it. My turn to drive.

CLOSE UP - KIMBERLY SCREAMS!
AND WE'RE BACK
THE HIGHWAY ON RAMP
Sweating profuscly, Kimberly's eyes dart around, taking in her surroundings.

DANO (O.S.)
Flight 180. Y'know, that plane crash with those kids from Mt.
Abraham?
The Old Woman BUMPS the window - scaring the shit out of everyone.
The kids ad-lib "Let's go", "Fucking freak."
Kimberly stares in horror as the Old Woman flashes an evil grin.
Kimberly's eyes lower to the bag of oranges, which breaks, exactly like before and the
Old Woman scurries after them.
The signal turns from red to flashing yellow.

FRANKIE
Dano, shouldn't we stop and help your mother?

DANO
Blow me. Yellow mcans go, Kimmy.
Kimberly hyperventilates in the driver's seat. Freaking. A yellow mini- bus with football
players speeds by.

KIMBERLY
Oh my God, oh my God...
Dano, confused, rolls a joint.

SHAINA
What is it? What are you?

KIMBERLY
There's going to be a huge accident! Everyone's gonna die, all of us, I saw it!
Dano hums the Twilight Zone theme.

FRANKIE
That's it. My turn to drive.
HONK! The drivers behind them start leaning on their horns. Kimberly leans out the window and sees the Chevette, the Pacer, The White Van, the Trans Am, the Harley...all the familiar vehicles from the pile up. She turns on the radio, frantically scans the dial.

SHAINA
Relax, you need to chill the fuck out.

KIMBERLY
Highway to Hell, Highway to Hell.

SHAINA
For Christ sakes girl, take a breath.

D.J. (O.S.)
Taking you into an all request weekend with a classic from AC/DC.
The opening guitar riff to HIGHWAY TO HELL blares from the speakers.
Kimberly turns to Shaina with a "believe me know?" look, but Shaina's nowhere near on the same page.
HONKING behind them.
Kimberly, shaking like a leaf, pulls the SUV forwards, turning it sideways to block off all traffic.

DANO
What the hell are you doing?
Dano shifts in his seat and sees - a Highway Pat rol Car ominously cruising up the shoulder of the onramp. He shoves a bag of weed, along with the joint, down his pants.

DANO
Five-O's coming! Let's fucking roll, man!
Officer Thomas Burke stops the car behind them.

FRANKIE
Jesus Christ! Here he comes!
Move!

KIMBERLY

No! We'll all die if we do!
The cop turns on his FLASHERS.

DANO
I told you she'd ruin everything!

SHAINA
Shut up, Dano, just stay cool.
(to Kimberly)
He's just stoned.
Officer Thomas Burke exits his car and approaches the passenger side of the SUV, hand on weapon. Thomas taps the window with his knuckle.

THOMAS
What's going on here?

KIMBERLY
(incoherent, through tears)
There's going to be a pile up.
Logs. Bodies everywhere. I saw it happen. It happened.
Thomas looks to the guys in back who shrug, "we don't know her."

THOMAS
Miss, please step out of the vehicle.
As she does, Thomas discretely unsnaps his holster. RORY nervously eyes the action. Sneaks a paper bundle into his sock. ISABELLA, the pregnant woman in the White Van, gets out. She gives Thomas her friendliest smile, milking the pregnant belly.

ISABELLA
Excuse me, but is there some way we could just drive around? I have a delivery.
Her CELL PHONE RINGS and she leans back inside to answer it.

ISABELLA
Hey hon, you got a mysterious caller on the answering machine from Planned Parenthood. What's going on?
As she listens, growing agitated, the Harley Rider dismounts and pulls off his helmet. Revealing EUGENE DIX, 35, a nebbishy school teacher in cool leathers.

INSIDE PACER
NORA watches the SUV, distressed.

NORA
What on Earth are they doing?

TIM
(picking up two Naya bottles)

Who am I, David Blane?
Nora gives Tim a hard stare, then they both break into smiles. Nora tousles his hair.
And doesn't stop.

TIM
(good-natured laughter)
Okay, quit it already.
As he laughs, something pains his jaw and he winces. THOMAS isn't quite sure what
kind of insanity he's dealing with yet. Dano and
Frankie, no help, stare dead ahead.

KIMBERLY
(trying to calm herself)
The radio played the same songs, the old lady's bag broke the exact same way it did in
my premonition.
Kimberly erupts into a panic when she sees the LOG TRUCK speed past.
She grabs at Thomas for emphasis.

KIMBERLY
THAT's the truck that's going to kill everyone!

THOMAS
Alright miss, calm down. I just need this lane open. I need you to pull your vehicle onto
the shoulder!

KIMBERLY
You're not listening to me! You have to do something!
EVAN impatiently yells out the window of his TRANS AM.

EVAN
Arrest this whack-job, wouldja?
Some of us have lives, y'know.
Kimberly looks to Shaina for support, but even Shaina can't meet her eyes.

KIMBERLY
Why won't anyone listen to me?
Thomas, subtly reaching for his cuffs.

THOMAS
I'm not going to tell you to calm down again
A SERIES OF CRASHES AND EXPLOSIONS ARE HEARD. In the distance. It's
neverending. Horrific. Kimberly's face crumbles. She screams in horror and collapses
against the SUV.
Thomas runs to his patrol car.
The White Delivery Van makes a J- turn out of the line of cars and
SPEEDS down the onramp in reverse, Isabella screaming angrily into her cell phone.

ISABELLA
You couldn't keep your dick in check for a month?!
The other drivers exit their cars, craning their necks to see what's happened up ahead.
Kat takes a deep drag off her smoke.

KAT
Great, now I'm really gonna be late.
Thomas barks into the radio handset

THOMAS
L.A. 51, I need assistance and requesting paramedics for a major
T.A. At

INSIDE THE SUV
Frankie watches the traffic start to back up as a couple of passing cars BRAKE HARD.
Shaina anxiously watches Kimberly pacing behind the

SUV.
SHAINA
Kimberly, what's going on?
Kimberly moves toward Shaina's window. As she leans her head into
Shaina's window, an ominous BREEZE blows back their hair and we hear the
BLARING HORN of a TRUCK.
And Kimberly is unexpectedly yanked backward by Thomas!
From nowhere, a SHRIEK of BRAKES as a JACK-KNIFED TRUCK plow s the SUV
across the frame! CRASH! Flying debris misses Kimberly and Thomas by inches!
Kimberly cries in horror into Thomas' shoulder as her friends burn up in the wreckage.

EXT. POLICE STATION - ESTABLISHING SHOT
INT. POLICE STATION - CONTINUOUS
CHAOS. Evan, the driver of the Trans Am, impatiently speaks to
DETECTIVE SUBY, late 40s, professional with an open face that makes him a great
listener.

EVAN
I don't know what you want from me.
Some crazy chic k blocks the highway with her car, said there'd be an accident and there
was. Big deal.
Even a broken watch is right twice a day...
Officer Thomas Burke passes by, heading into

INT. A ROOM - CONTINUOUS
Kat, Eugene, Nora, Tim, and Rory sit in a large room, waiting to give statements. Unlike
Evan, these witnesses are clearly distraught.

KAT
Not to sound insensitive, but how much longer is this going to take?

EUGENE
If I don't get back to my classroom soon, the kids'll tear the room apart.

NORA
Those poor people. To think it would've been us if not for...
PAN OVER TO REVEAL KIMBERLY. She's still in shock, her mind far away.
Thomas sits close to her, speaking softly.

THOMAS
Tell me again how it started.

KIMBERLY
Like I said, it was like I was there. I remember everything. The sounds of the crashes,
the smells, the look on Shaina's face...

THOMAS
Do you remember what triggered it all?

KIMBERLY
The log truck...and everybody I guess. Everyone was driving like a maniac. And
somehow I knew something horrible was going to happen, even before it did.
Something clicks for Thomas, but he forces himself to speak calmly, like a lawyer
leading a friendly witness.

THOMAS
You knew? You just mean a hunch, right? A bad vibe, maybe?
The other drivers stare at Kimberly.

KIMBERLY
More than that. All the songs on the radio were about car crashes.
Some kid's banging toy cars together.
(lookin g at her)
She was dialing her cell phone with her headset on.
(points to Rory)
His car was leaking oil all over the road.

RORY
Hey, don't be knockin' the
Chevette.
But the others listen intently now. Especially Kat, who spies her headset buried deep in
her purse.

KIMBERLY

Billboards about accidents. Kids yelling "pile up" for no reason.
It all felt...just wrong.
Just like...
(swallows; hesitates)

THOMAS
Like what?
Kimberly sighs and looks down. The room becomes eerily silent, except for the FLICKER of a florescent light.

KIMBERLY
I know this sounds crazy...but you all heard about Flight 180, right?
The kid who got off the plane?
Thomas' eyes widen then a startling CRASH as Rory, le aning back in his chair, tips over. Thomas rolls his eyes as Rory grins sheepishly and picks himself up.

THOMAS
You mean Alex Browning.

KIMBERLY
(looking down)
...My Premonition was just like his.

NORA
What are you talking about?

EUGENE
(sarcastic)
Oh, you must have read about that kid who had a dream about a plane crash so he got his buddies off the plane? Then the thing blew up just like in the dream?

NORA
Maybe...
Eugene sees Nora and Tim are hooked and speaks in scary campfire tones.

EUGENE
But this is where it starts to get freaky. So a month goes by, everything seems cool, but then the survivors start dying one boy one.
'Cause when your number's up, it's up, right? Some people said Death itself started coming for them, hunting down every last one, until they were all dead.
Everyone tenses up.

THOMAS
Well, not quite all of them. Clear
Rivers checked herself into a padded room at Stoneybrook.
Kimberly, affected, looks to Thomas for confirmation.

KIMBERLY
You do believe me, don't you?
BANG! Everyone jumps as Detective Suby pounds on the door and opens it.

DETECTIVE SUBY
Officer Burke? Could I see you in here?

INT. OBSERVATION ROOM - CONTINUOUS
The DOOR OPENS. Detective Suby enters, leading Thomas. Through a two - way mirror, they can see the others chatting anxiously.

DETECTIVE SUBY
Tell me you didn't start up on that
Flight 180 shit again.
(beat)
Did you?

THOMAS
Of course not. That would be irresponsible and unprofessional.
Detective Suby's persistent glare makes Thomas uncomfortable.

THOMAS
Look, you weren't there. It was weird. She knew that log truck was gonna cause an accident, she knew.
(beat)
Never mind.

DETECTIVE SUBY
I thought we we re finished with this bullshit. This is police work, not the psychic Hot Line.
But Thomas isn't listening. He's glued to Kimberly's words. When Detective Suby realizes this, he stops and listens.

KIMBER LY
But if I was never meant to pull over, then we all should have died in the pile up.

TIM
Which means Death could be coming for us.
Detective Suby looks pissed o ff.

DETECTIVE SUBY
Way to console the witnesses Burke.
At the same time, we watch Evan enter the other room, grab his jacket and wave goodbye to the others.

DETECTIVE SUBY
You got 'em thinking Death is after them? Shit, they're the luckiest sons o' bitches on the planet. Get this guy Evan Shaeffer; Yesterday the kid wins the lotto and today some looney bitch b locks traffic and he avoids the worst pile up in years. I should be so damn unlucky.

INT. A ROOM - CONTINUOUS
Kimberly, Nora, Tim, Kat, Eugene and Rory now seem affected by what they've heard.

KAT
What if it's true? What if it's happening all over again?
The fluorescent light above FLICKERS ominously. Nora, disturbed, stands up in a huff, grabbing Tim's arm.

NORA
You're all certifiable, you know that? I can't believe I've been listening to this crap. Come on,
Tim, let's go outside.

TIM
Jeez, Mom, stop trippin'.

EUGENE
Look lady, we're just yankin' your chain.

RORY
Yeah, you're acting like we all just got the Diff'rent Strokes curse or something.
Eugene and Rory burst out laughin g. Nora shakes her head, disgusted.

NORA
What's wrong with you people?
Nora pulls a reluctant Tim out of the room. As she opens the door, the others watch Detective Suby and Thomas appear from nowhere to calm her down . When the door swings shut, an awkward silence.
Suddenly, the door opens again and Thomas leads Mr. Burroughs inside.
Mr. Burroughs sees Kimberly and chokes back tears.

MR. BURROUGHS
Kimberly...
The sight of her fath er crying is cnough to make Kimberly's own dam burst. She rushes over to him and buries her head in his chest, sobbing.

MR. BURROUGHS
Can I take her home?
Thomas nods.

DETECTIVE SUBY
Sure, you can all go.
By now, the fluorescent light flickers out of control. When Rory, Kat and Eugene stand up, Thomas looks helpless.

KAT
First I'm stuck with Jury Duty, now this nonsense.

RORY
Yeah, I hate to love and leave ya, but I've been over this X-Files shit since the sixth season.
As Thomas watches them file out, the fluorescent light POPS. Then

DARKNESS.
INT. KITCHEN - DAY
Kimberly sits at the table. Mr. Burroughs sets down a cup of tea before her. Both are shaken.

KIMBERLY
I know it's crazy, but I'm really scared for the others. I've got this terrible feeling.

MR. BURROUGHS
What feeling?

KIMBERLY
That it's not over yet.
She picks up the tea, it clatters in her trembling hands.

MR. BURROUGHS
Don 't worry. Everything will be fine, you'll see.

INT. EVAN'S STAIRWELL - DAY
A dingy singly light bulb illuminates the narrow stairwell. Evan appears in the darkness, carrying a brand new television with some packages on top. He's unable to s ee the long rickety stairwell he climbs.
The stairs are littered with Chinese take out MENUS and a TONKA TRUCK apparently left by some kids.
As Evan slowly climbs the staircase, a FAT MAN comes down, forcing
Evan to lean against -
THE RAILING - which CREAKS and BENDS. After the FAT MAN passes, Evan slowly continues up again, TEARING HIS SHIRT on a nail.

EVAN
Motherfucker.
A HEATING DUCT CLICKS ON. The air blows a TONKA TRUCK slowly toward the center of the staircase, directly in Evan's path - but Evan just misses it!

He continues past MORE TOYS, nearing the top stair -
The Airduct coughs, sending menus fluttering toward Evan's feet and he slips on them!
He juggles the TV - but ultimately rights himself and continues down the hallway.

INT. EVAN'S APARTMENT - CONTINUOUS
Dim, cheap, probably roach-infested. As Evan enters, the small packages fall off the TV box and onto the floor.
Evan places the TV by the door, looks at his torn shirt, but fuck it, who cares; he's on a natural high. He peels his shirt off, revealing his PIERCED NIPPLES, flicks on the radio and DANCES his way over to the fridge and grabs a drink.
In the tiny kitchenette area, a small swarm of flies hovers over a grease-filled frying pan.
Evan recoils, throws open the window and throws the grease to the sidewalk five stories below. An ominous BREEZE enters
And a kitchen cabinet slowly BLOWS OPEN. Some FORKS and KNIVES slide forward on poorly stacked plates. Daring to fall into the toaster.
Evan spills some cooking oil on the range while pouring it into the frying pan, then dumps in some frozen mozzarella sticks. Evan puts the frying pan on the stove and turns it on HIGH.
He then grabs a container of CHINESE FOOD and rests it on the counter next to the fridge. On the fridge, several colorful MAGNETS spell out

HEY E.
PUSH IN on the H - which mysteriously drops into the Chinese food - the word EY E remaining. Oblivious, Evan puts the food in the microwave and turns it on.

ANGLE ON STOVE
The cooki ng oil creeps toward the range... Evan hits PLAY on his answering machine and rushes across the room to tear open his packages...

VOICE (O.S.)
Dude! You suck! You buy one fucking ticket in your whole life and win twenty grand? We're going whoring in Prague, you know this!
(whisper)
Hold on, the boss is coming.
A CLICK, then hold MUZAK: AC/DC's HIGHWAY TO HELL.
ANGLE ON MAGNET in Chinese fo od. SPARKING. It pops and fizzles. And ugly sound.
As many similar messages continue, Evan unwraps a new ROLEX! He slides it over his wrist, admiring it.

ANGLE ON KNIFE
Lazily sliding off the shelf and into the toaster, protruding about an inch and a half. Hardly noticeable.
By now, Evan has opened the next package; a gaudy gold and diamond encrusted horseshoe ring.

He carries the ring into the kitchenette, sees the Chinese food is
FLAMING, and his hands flash out to turn it off A SMALL EXPLOSION from the
microwave startles him.
The RING falls into his drain/garbage disposal!

EVAN
Damn it!
Evan reaches INTO THE DRAIN, his fingers searching for the ring. When he tries to
pull his hand back out, the ROLEX CATCHES.
Another small EXPLOSION from the microwave, this one cracking the
GLASS. A Solo Plastic Cup nearby begins to melt.
Flames sputter around the rim of the frying pan. In moments, the oil from the pan
IGNITES. A small fire.
Evan sees all this and YANKS with all his might. No use. As the FIRE slowly spreads
to nearby cereal boxes, Evan starts to panic. He continues yanking... Stuck.
He sees a bottle of PALMOLIVE on the other end of the counter. His fingers reach for
it.
Slightly out of his grasp. But his fingertips are just long enough to knock the bottle
backwards - where it rests against TWO SWITCHES.
The FIRE ALARM goes off. The PHONE RINGS.
Evan desperately lifts his leg and tries to use his foot to edge the
Palmolive over. By pushing the bottle up against the wall, it threatens to turn on one of
the switches.

ANGLE ON FINGERS
In the GARBAGE DISPOSAL. A SWITCH is flipped - but the light goes on.
And the Palmolive lazily falls, resting on the remaining switch.

EVAN
Come on, come on...
Evan makes one last push with his foot - accidently flipping the
SWITCH - the GARBAGE DISPOSAL GRINDS METAL!
Evan, horrified, miraculously yanks his hand free, brushing against the knife in the
toaster.
When the SHOCK goes through Evan's body, his other hand jerks out, knocking the
flaming frying pan to the floor.
The entire kitchen is in flames, including the new TV blocking the door. The window
slams SHUT! The room fills with smoke.

EVAN
Jesus Christ!
Evan grabs a fire extinguisher. A mere dribble of foam comes out. He begins
COUGHING in the smoke.
Evan tries the window - STUCK! He has no choice but to smash the kitchenette window
with the fire extinguisher to get to the fire escape.

He dr ops the fire extinguisher, starts to climb out the window, hears a creak and looks up just as

A large jagged shard of glass comes CRASHING down at him Evan jumps back just in time as it shatters before him. The fire completely engulfs the kitchen.

He bravely jumps through the window pane, landing on the fire escape.

He runs down the fire escape from floor to floor.

A LARGE BLAST from his window showers him with glass and brick shrapnel, but ultimately, he makes it to the fire escape's lowest level, intact.

He tries to lower the rusty metal ladder to the ground. It budges once, then twice, but won't go down. So he climbs over the railing and gently drops to the ground.

Safe and sound, he breathes a sigh of relief and turns to walk

SUDDENLY he s lips on the very grease he threw out the window, his legs shoot out from under him and he lands on his back.

The rusty ladder suddenly dislodges and hurls downward coming right for Evan's face but stops halfway!

As Evan laughs, breathing a final sigh of relief, it suddenly

PLUMMETS again impaling Evan through his eye socket!

INT. POLICE STATION - COMPUTER ROOM - NIGHT

Thomas sits at the computer terminal. He checks to make sure no one's watching as he enters a SEARCH for Alex Browning.

Ten websites come up, all devoted to the Flight 180 Curse. Thomas scrolls around, seeing the death pix and autopsy photos of Flight 180 "survivors".

Headlines blare, "Freak Accident?" "Bizarre Coincidence?" describing the way the victims died. As Thomas begins a localized search of the word, "PREMONITION"

SPOOKY HUMMING from behind him.

Thomas whirls around to see Det. Suby looking over his shoulder, humming the music from an old monster movie. Suby presses one hand to his forehead, the other polishing an apple against his vest.

DETECTIVE SUBY
(as if entranced)
Ooooh, I see it now. Your future... A transfer to another department.

Suby bites the apple, casually offering nothing more. Thomas, embarrassed, flicks off the computer, stands.

THOMAS
You've made your point.

DETECTIVE SUBY
Good. Cause we just got some new info and I don't ne ed you getting freaky on me.

THOMAS
What?

DETECTIVE SUBY
Evan Shaeffer's dead. Guess he wasn't as lucky as we thought.
Detective Suby shrugs and walks away, munching the apple. Thomas looks stunned.

INT. KAT'S ROOM - NIGHT
Kat cradles a phone to her shoulder. She watches television and crushes Oreos into a bowl of ice- cream.

KAT
No, Mom. Just turn on any station, they've been playing it all day.
(beat; rolls her eyes)
Yes, Mother. Channel four will do just fine. Here it is, gotta go.
She hangs up the phone, mesmerized by the report:
FOOTAGE FROM A HELICOPTER shows the pile up wreckage.

ANCHOR MAN (V.O.)
Route 18 was backed up for almost nine hours today when a record breaking pile up...

INT. NORA'S LIVING ROOM - CONTINUOUS
Nora and Tim watch the same report.

ANCHOR MAN (V.O.)
...killed An estimated 18 people.
Emergency crews spent hours sifting through the wreckage.

INT. EUGENE'S LIVING ROOM - CONTINUOUS
Eugene looks up from grading midterm bluebooks to watch.

ANCHOR MAN (V.O.)
...hoping To recover any survivors from this tragic collision. So far, the police are refusing to release the names of the victims until their families are notified.

INT. KIMBERLY'S HOUSE - CONTINUOUS
Mr. Burroughs numbly watches the same report. He doesn't see Kimberly enter behind him from the kitchen.

ANCHOR WOMAN (O.S.)
The camera of a highway patrol car managed to catch this shocking footage
B/W CAMERA FOOTAGE from Thomas' car shows Thomas tackling Kimberly to the ground just as a jack -knifed truck plows into the SUV.

MR. BURROUGHS
My Lord...
A GASP from behind him. Mr. Burroughs spins to see Kimberly fighting back tears and picks up the remote, prepared to click of the TV but she stops him.

KIMBERLY
Don't. I have to see this.
Mr. Burroughs reluctantly keeps the newscast on.

INT. RORY'S APARTMENT - CONTINUOUS
It's a party. Rory, surrounded by BUDDIES, shakes a triumphant fist at the television.
HE WHOOPS with delight, spilling popcorn everywhere.

RORY
Whoohoo! You see that shit? Right there? That's my fuckin' car right there! Oh God, that's dope.
After high-fiving his peeps, he bends to table level and snorts a freshly chopped line.

ANCHOR MAN (O.S.)
In other news, a freak accident took the life of a lotto winner.
Rory looks up to see the DMV photo of Evan. As he takes in the report, his mood radically shifts. He looks like he's been hit by a train.

MONTAGE
Of Kimberly, Nora, Tim, Eugene and Kat watching. They all take the news very hard as the FOOTAGE shows Evan's BODY being carried away by
EMT workers. Eugene, however, shakes his head sadly but goes back to grading blue books.

TIM'S BEDROOM - LATER
Tim's eyes are glued to the latest Stephen King novel. Nora peers in.

NORA
Come on, Tim, lights out already.
Tim starts at her voice, then reluctantly puts down the book.

TIM
Mom?

NORA
Yeah?

TIM
You think... You think those guys were b.s.-ing us today or what?
Nora swallows, trying to seem brave.

NORA
Oh, please. Some people just need some serious rewiring, that's all.
But neither of them are convinced.

NORA

Get some sleep.
Nora kisses his forehead and leaves the room. After she leaves, Tim opens his nightstand drawer, pulls out a dusty nightlight and plugs it in.

INT. NORA'S BEDROOM - MOMENTS LATER
Nora closes her bedroom door. And locks it. She nervously checks the closet and even lowers the blinds. Finally, she takes out a business card and dials a number. She hangs up, then dials again.

NORA
Officer Burke, please?

INT. KIMBERLY'S ROOM - CONTINUOUS
Mr. Burroughs tucks a still-shaken Kimberly into bed. In one of his hands is a nearly empty glass of scotch.

KIMBERLY
It's okay, Dad. I'm not ten anymore.
Mr. Burroughs catches himself being overprotective.

MR. BURROUGHS
I'm sorry. I'm just so happy that you're safe.

KIMBERLY
I love you too, Dad. Goodnight.
But Mr. Burroughs isn't ready to leave. He finishes his drink.

MR. BURROUGHS
You know, after your mother died...
Kimberly tenses, bracing for the worst.

MR. BURROUGHS
There were so many times I didn't think I could last another day. I can't even tell you some of the things I th ought about.

KIMBERLY
I used to have those feelings, too.
But that's when I'd think of Mom.
Her strength...and courage. And
I'd pray that maybe I'd grow up to be as brave as she was. And the bad thoughts would go away.

MR. BURROUGHS
(choking up)
I don't know what I'd do if I lost you.

Mr. Burroughs leans over, kisses her forehead and leaves. Just as he's out the door, he braces at the distant sound of a CAR SKIDDING out of control. The ENDLESS SCREECH is nerve shattering. Mr.
Burroughs stands frozen, tensing for the inevitable crunch. But there is none. And he leaves.

DISSOLVE TO:
INT. KIMBERLY'S ROOM - NIGHT
The room is dark except for one burning candle. Kimberly tosses and turns. The wind sends a single branch scraping against her window. A porch swing SQUEAKS back and forth. Adding to her anxiety.
A BREEZE ENTERS, sputtering out the candle. Kimberly sits upright in bed and sees the WINDOW IS SHUT. Huh? She lights a match and sees the candle wax dripped onto her table, forming the gooey shape of a...180? The match goes out in her hand. The room is dark again.
Headlights fr om passing cars cast eerie shadows on her ceiling.
Shadows resembling PLANES seem to transform into a SKULL.
Kimberly, freaked out, looks around to see the blinking light from the VCR: it flashes 18:0 a few times, then 12:00.
She can't take it anymore. She yanks the VCR cord from the wall and flicks on the lights, ridding the room of shadows. And anxiously turns on her computer.

EXT. STONEYBROOK HOSPITAL - DAY
Kimberly drives a beat up Hyundai through an eerie morning mist that surrounds the grounds of the Stoneybrook Hospital.

ANGLE ON
A computer printout in the shotgun seat: MAPQUEST directions to
"Stoneybrook Hospital".
As Kimberly drives through the gate, the mist almost seems to follow her inside.
A SIGN offers a choice between "Emergency/Medica l Care" or
"Psychiatric Treatment Center." Kimberly drives to the mental ward.

INT. MENTAL WARD - DAY
A PHYSICIAN in a lab coat leads a nervous Kimberly down the center of a long corridor. The Physician consults a clipboard.

PHYSICIAN

...at the request of the patient, you are to relinquish any sharp objects such as nail files, pencils, pens, safety pins, bobby pins, no matches, lighters, belts, belt buckles, earrings, chokers, shoelaces...
Kimberly watches carefully as the Physician comes to a door and punches "4514" into the electronic lock. They continue down another corridor.
Lights flicker,patients cackle and moan in the B.G.

PHYSICIAN

...paper clips, watches, food, drinks, keys, poisons, pills and medications.
(looks at Kimberly)
You have a cell phone on you?
Kimberly nods, hands it over.

PHYSICIAN
Then I think we're all done.
They arrive at a door to a padded room. The Physician punches in another code.

KIMBERLY
Wait. Is she...dangerous or something?

PHYSICIAN
No honey, but she expects you are.

KIMBERLY
Jesus, how long are you going to keep her locked up this way?

PHYSICIAN
Depends on her, I guess. She's voluntary.
The door hisses open.

INT. CLEAR'S PADDED ROOM - CONTINUOUS
REVEAL CLEAR RIVERS
While still beautiful, this young woman bears few traces of her former self. Her eyes
dart around suspiciously, maddened by chronic paranoia. Her hair is patchy, her eyes
dark and haunted. Bordering on savage. Her movements are fidgety, erratic, always
distracted by something unseen.

KIMBERLY
Clear Rivers?
Clear looks Kimberly up and down and steps back, allowing her inside her inner
sanctum. A mattress on the floor, a plastic bottle of water, some paperbacks and a
bedpan.
Kimberly's jaw drops when she sees the far wall: a SHRINE to flight
180. The wall is papered with art icles about all the survivors (as seen in the opening
title montage).
The door SLAMS. Kimberly jumps.

CLEAR
Kimberly Burroughs, eh? What do you want?

KIMBERLY
I thought...I thought you might be able to help me.

CLEAR

(snicker)
Yeah, how?

KIMBERLY
I had a premonition about the Route
18 pile up. .. I saved some people.
And now I think Death is after me.

CLEAR
Nice work. Maybe if you're real lucky, you'll wind up in here with me.
(gives Kimberly the once over)
But I doubt you'll survive that long.
Kimberly flinches.

KIMBERLY
It's not just about me. Someone I saved died last night in a freak accident. What if the others are in danger, too?

CLEAR
Well, if you put them on the list, they're already tits up.

KIMBERLY
What list?

CLEAR
Death's list. The precise order you're going to die in.
Clear's eyes bore into a terrified Kimberly's.

CLEAR
The survivors of Flight 180 died in the exact order they were originally meant to die in the plane crash. That was Death's original design.

KIMBERLY
(sudden realization)
Exact order? Then I'm next! I was meant to die with my friends, so
I'm next!
Clear backs away from Kimberly as if she were lethal, then stops short.

CLEAR
But you said someone else died last night. That means Death skipped past you. Someone must have intervened.
(off Kimberly's confusion)
Sometime yesterday you must have nearly died, but someone saved you.
Kimberly nods, recalling the events.

KIMBERLY

Officer Burke pulled me away from the crash that killed my friends.

CLEAR
Congratufuckinglations. That makes you last to go. But don't worry, once the others are dead, it'll come back for you. Always does.

KIMBERLY
That still doesn't make sense. You said you die in the same order you were originally meant to. But Evan
Shaeffer died last in my premonition, not first.
Clear seems very disturbed by that.

CLEAR
It's moving backwards? Are you sure?
Kimberly reluctantly strains to remember something...

HARD CUT TO:
THE FINAL MOMENTS OF THE PILE UP
Nora's Pacer folds like an accordion, then EXPLODES, followed by Evan screaming in the Trans Am, which gets CREAMED by the semi!

BACK TO:
Kimberly, shaken, does the math.

KIMBERLY
Yes. In my premonition that Nora woman and her kid died first, then
Evan and then...my friends.
Clear is oblivious when Kimberly breaks into silent sobs.

CLEAR
Backwards...that's new.
Clear sees Kimberly crying and softens.

CLEAR
That's good. Get all your tears out now, you'll need your eyes.
(off Kimberly's confusion)
For the signs.

KIMBERLY
Signs?

CLEAR
If you have the same power as Alex, you'll be seeing signs soon. When you see anything creepy or ominous, an in-your- face irony kinda thing?
Don't ignore it. It usually means the difference between life and death.

KIMBERLY
(to herself)
The songs on the radio.
(to Clear)
But wait. I don't understand. Why is this even happening to me?

CLEAR
That's what Alex used to ask himself right up until...
For an instant, we see a gentle side of Clear.

KIMBERLY
It's obvious you know what you're talking about. You beat it. You have to help us.
Clear suddenly toughens up, an abrupt mood shift.

CLEAR
I didn't beat it; I hid from it.
If you were smart you'd put a down payment on a burial plot and say goodbye to the dog, because what little life you have left is over as you know it. Don't make new friends, don't fall in love, and don't ever bother trying to save others. That's the worst killer of them all.

KIMBERLY
How can you say that? What kind of monster are you?
At once, Clear, enraged, is in her face, speaking through clenched teeth.

CLEAR
My family is dead. My friends are dead. And Alex...
Clear angrily peels a Polaroid off the wall and shows it to Kimberly.
While we don't see the photo, Kimberly's horrified face paints a gruesome picture on its own.

CLEAR
And yes, that's the blade of a fucking ceiling fan in his head.
Clear pounds on the door, apparently done with Kimberly. A GUARD opens the door.
Kimberly, devastated, turns to leave, then summons her courage and turns back to Clear.

KIMBERLY
Know what? I think you're a coward. I think you hide out in here because you're too damn bitter and selfish to care about another living soul. In my opinion, you're already dead.
Kimberly leaves, giving Clear something to think about.

EXT. KIMBERLY'S HOUSE - DAY
As Kimberly pulls into her driveway, she's surprised to see a STRANGE
CAR parked there. Then

THOMAS, wearing street clothes, peers through the front window of the house. He guiltily backs away as Kimberly gets out.

THOMAS
I tried calling last night but your father

KIMBERLY
Evan Shaeffer's dead.
Thoma s nods and leans against the large glass windows that reflect the sky behind them.

THOMAS
I know. I've gotten calls all morning from everyone who was on the onramp. We're all meeting at my apartment tonight.

KIMBERLY
Then you believe all this?? That
Death is working off a list?
Thomas hesitates before answering.

THOMAS
I didn't. Until I was dispatched to clean up one of the Flight 180 survivors.

KIMBERLY
Clean up? I don't...
Suddenly through the reflection of the window glass, Kimberly sees hundreds of pigeons dive bomb her at once!
Like a scene out of THE BIRDS, Kimberly must duck and cover as the pigeons assault her from every angle.
But when Kimberly turns away from the reflection, toward the actual pigeons, THEY'RE GONE. ALL IN HER HEAD.

KI MBERLY
Did you see that??
Thomas, concerned for her, saw nothing.

KIMBERLY
Pigeons... It's a sign! If Clear's right about the order, then Nora and Tim are going to be attacke d by
Pigeons!

THOMAS
I'm not following you

KIMBERLY
They're next on the list. We have to find them.

EXT. MEDICAL COMPLEX - DAY
ANGLE ON
Woman's N ike shoe on a down-moving escalator. Reveal Nora taking her son Tim to a dentist's office. The SHOELACE snags on a bolt of one of the steel side panels, untying it...

TIM
(mischievous smile)
You think the tooth fairy's gonna come tonight? I'm thinkin' like fifteen bucks.

NORA
Nice try, kiddo.
Tim smiles, then winces from the pain in his mouth.
THE DANGLING SHOELACE heads straight for the escalator grate. IT GETS SWALLOWED UP. As Tim steps off, Nora TRIPS forward. Her caught sneaker is pulled tighter into the innards of the metal staircase.

TIM
Mom!
Tim watches helplessly as Nora reaches down, tug ging at her sneaker, fear mounting. Tim also grabs her sneaker and yanks. Finally, the shoelace SNAPS, and Nora's free again.

TIM
You okay?
Nora puts on a brave face and begins tying one long shoelace to the stubby one.

NORA
Sure hon. I'm fine. Let's shake it, we're late.
Tim nods. The wind picks up as they continue past a

CONSTRUCTION CREW
Who apply industrial suction cups to large, thick sheets of PLATED

GLASS .
Tim stares in childlike fascination as they pass JACKHAMMERS, a CEMENT MIXER, and an EXCAVATOR.

INT. CLEAR'S PADDED ROOM - DAY
Clear Rivers applies fun- tack to the back of a newspaper article and sticks it on the wall devoted to Flight 180.

REVEAL
A photo of Eva, "Lotto Winner Killed By Ladder".

Clear backs away, pausing to look at a group photo of the Survivors of Flight 180 just before take off. Smiling faces.

TIM
Not so much.
Dr. Lees keeps a skeptical smile to himself.

INT. WAITING ROOM - CONTINUOUS
The RECEPTIONIST appears next to the fallen fish food with a VACUUM.
She plugs it in an outlet below the fishtank.
A startling GRIND as the vacuum turns on and coughs up a nail. She vacuums up the fish food around Nora's feet.
The DEAD FISH gets sucked into the water filter in the fishtank which sputters and stops. The water level RISES, spilling water over the side of the tank. The water TRICKLES closer to the outlet.

EXT. SUBURBAN STREET - DAY
Thomas drives his car into a friendly neighborhood. Kimberly, riding shotgun, hangs up her cell phone.

KIMBERLY
Turn around. The cleaning woman said they're at the dentist's.
14th and Main.

THOMAS
Hold on.
Thomas expertly skids into a U-turn.

INT. DENTIST OFFICE - CONTINUOUS
Tim looks petrified as Dr. Lees unveils a tray full of PICS, CARVERS and EXTRACTING FORCEPS.
The KA-CHUNG of construction outside makes it im possible to concentrate, but, hands trembling slightly, Dr. Lees picks up a pic and mirror and starts examining Tim's mouth. CU of PIC gently prodding Tim's teeth.

DR. LEES (O.S.)
I'm a little disappointed, Tim.
Does your mom know you've been smoking?
Tim groans "uh-uh", then suddenly flinches.

DR. LEES (O.S.)
Yeah, that'll have to be filled.
A BANG from the window startles Dr. Lees. His HAND JERKS, but luckily the pic was removed from Tim's mouth.
Dr. Lees whips around in time to see a PIGEON flutter away from the window.

DR. LEES
Jesus. Every day at the same damn time. Now this'll only sting for a moment.
Dr. Lees picks up a large SYRINGE and moves it toward Tim's open mouth.

DR. LEES
Open big. Wiiiiider...
Tim's eyes radiate fear. The MOUTH OPENS. Reluctantly. Tim nervously eyes the window as the needle enters...

ANGLE ON
NEEDLE heading toward his gumline
BANG! Another pigeon takes a header into the reflection. Dr. Lees' hand jerks, nearly jabbing Tim's tongue. Tim squirms violently. Dr.
Lees looks towards the window angrily.

DR. LEES
How the hell do they expect me to... Would you rather have the laughing gas?
Tim nods his head ferociously.

DR. LEES
Jean? I need you in here.
(waits)
Jean??!

INT. WAITING ROOM - CONTINUOUS
Jean continues vacuuming. The vacuum makes contact with Nora's foot.

INT. DENTIST OFFICE - CONTINUOUS
After a minute, Dr. Lees angrily switches on two compressors: Oxygen and Nitrous Oxide.
By now, the NO mask has been attached around Tim's nose. As Tim drifts off, Dr. Lees lowers a DRILL into his mouth.

DR. LEES
Open big. Wiiiiiider.
Excruciating SOUNDS of the drill going through enamel.

INTERCUT KIMBERLY AND THOMAS
Racing to the medical complex throughout.

THE WAITING ROOM
The WATER TRICKLES into the outlet. The vacuum sparks and dies just as

BACK IN DR. LEES' OFFICE
BANG! SFX: BROKEN GLASS - it sounds like a pigeon finally crashed through the window. In the other room.

DR. LEES
Goddamn it already.
Dr. Lees marches out of the room to investigate. Another quick electrical surge and the
OXYGEN COMPRESSOR flutters off. The needle drops. But the NITROUS flow
remains strong.

ANGLE ON FISH MOBILE
Spinning from a new breeze. Suddenly, a small round PUFFER FISH FALLS directly
into Tim's mouth.
Soft, gurgling and choking.

INT. WAITING ROOM - CONTINUOUS
Nora stares at a pigeon with a broken wing frantically trying to fly right. Dr. Lees makes
a half- hearted attempt to soothe and catch it.

BACK IN DR. LEES' OFFICE
SLOW DOLLY up to Tim. Choking, gurgling. His eyes are open, but rolled up. His
hand limply reaches up...then drops.
Sounds of commotion in the next room seem to fade away as we continue our SLOW
DOLLY into Tim's eyes.
They GLAZE OVER...the choking stops. And a HAND reaches into frame and pulls
the puffer fish out of Tim's mouth.
REVEAL JEAN looking petrified at the close call, looking around to make sure nobody
saw...

EXT. MEDICAL COMPLEX - LATER
Nora and Tim, feeling better now, walk past the CONSTRUCTION CREW. A
CRANE OPERATOR smiles at Tim, who smiles back.
From across the mall, the tiny running figures of Kimberly and Thomas appear in the
dis tance, pointing and screaming.

TIM
What are they doing here? And why are they yelling "pigeons"?
Just then, Tim and Nora walk into a large cluster of PIGEONS who suddenly burst into
flight, startling the Crane Operator, whose hand inadvertently jerks a lever -
A METALLIC CHAIN RATTLE fills the air and Tim looks up just as a HUGE
SHEET OF GLASS PLUMMETS downward toward him and CRUSHES him, his
mangled body visible underneath.
As two pearly whites roll around on the sidewalk, NORA SCREAMS.

DISSOLVE TO:
EXT. MEDICAL COMPLEX - LATER
Emergency vehicles everywhere. Thomas seems exhausted as he walks back to
Kimberly, who stands by his car. In the BG, EMTs load a stretcher into an ambulance.

THOMAS
(shaking his head)
Nora's not coming. She refuses to leave her son.

KIMBERLY
We have to tell her she's in danger!

THOMAS
(sadly)
I did. And right now, I don't think she cares.

EXT. KIMBERLY'S HOUSE - DAY
Thomas' car turns into the driveway and parks. Kimberly holds up her hand and watches it tremble.

KIMBERLY
It's happening again. It's fucking happening again. I hoped we'd get there and they'd be okay, that
Clear Rivers was full of shit and
Evan's death was just a freak accident...
Thomas kills the engine to listen.

KIMBERLY
But we're all going to die. We can't stop it. It's just a matter of time. I'm so scared.
Thomas takes her hand and squeeze s it reassuringly.

THOMAS
I am too. But you can use that fear. It'll sharpen your instincts. Keep you alert fro signs.
It's the only way you'll be able to sav e the others...and me.
Kimberly, seeming overwhelmed, pulls her hand back. Thomas senses he's losing her, and softens her approach.

THOMAS
I know you didn't ask for any of this, Kimberly. But I don't think you have it in you to quit either.
Kimberly stares straight ahead, the weight of the world sinking in.
BANG! A startling pound on the roof of Thomas' car.
Kimberly jumps, then spins around to see:
CLEAR RIVERS - standing in the driveway. A determined, powerful presence.
Kimberly exits the car. A MOMENT where Kimberly and Clear stare each other down.

KIMBERLY
Clear/Thomas. Thomas/Clear.
Clear nods absently to Thomas, still focused on Kimberly.

KIMBERLY

(bitter)
The second one just dies. A 16 year old kid.

CLEAR
(nods; a faint trace of guilt)
I hope you're ready for this.

EXT. FUNERAL HOME - DAY
Thomas' car pulls into a partially filled parking lot. Kimberly,
Thomas and Clear file out and head to the door.

KIMBERLY
This is cheery.

THOMAS
Who is this guy, anyway?

CLEAR
A mortician. He seemed to know a hell of a lot more about death than he ever told us.

THOMAS
Should we knock?

CLEAR
(looking ill)
He probably already knows we're coming.

INT. FUNERAL HOME - MOMENTS LATER
Kimberly, Thomas and Clear open the large wooden doors into a small chapel, creat ing
a loud CREAK. A corpse in an open casket sits at the front of the chapel, post -wake.
Kimberly, Thomas and Clear are forced to walk around the dead body to get to a side
door.

INT. CORRIDOR - MOMENTS LATER
The three slowly edge towards a room at the end of a creepy hallway.
An ORANGE GLOW flickers from the far room. The unmistakable sounds of a furnace
make it all the more eerie.
As they near the door, they're able to see inside the room; the shadow of a figure looms
against a steel oven.
They edge closer. They peek inside the

INT. CREMATORIUM
Oddly there is no one there. As they enter, passing the furnace, a momentary WHOOSH
of flames startles them all!
They jump back - bumping right into:

MR. BLUDWORTH, the dark, sinister mortician from FD1, who has inexplicably appear BEHIND THEM.

MORTICIAN
Hello, Clear. I've been keeping an eye out for you.
The mortician rolls a metal gurney carrying EVAN'S EYELESS BODY toward the firing oven. Kimberly and Thomas are scared.

KIMBERLY
Oh my God. That's Evan Shaeffer.
Clear, however, seems to expect nothing less.

MORTICIAN
Come to... Pick my brain?
The Mortician slides a gleaming set of medical pliers into Evan's mouth. And YANKS out a gold tooth. Kimberly recoils as he discards the bloody tooth on a metal tray.

MORTICIAN
(to Kimberly)
Flesh and bone require 1,600 degrees for cremation. Gold, prosthetics and other metals must be removed before the final

CLEAR
(not falling for this again)
Just a simple question and we'll leave you alone with your new friend.
The Mortician grins; he likes the new Clear. He crosses the room and hits a LEVER. KA- CHUNK! The oven begins to blaze.

MORTICIAN
Fire away.

CLEAR
How do you cheat Death once and for all?
The Mortician, recrossing the room, passes Kimberly and stoops down to sniff, no INHALE, a terrified Kimberly's essence.

MORTICIAN
Dead. But still fresh.
Kimberly shudders as the Mortician moves back to Evan's body. Clear has had about enough.

CLEAR
(to the Mortician)
Look, we drove a long way to get here. So if you happen to know how to get this death monkey off our backs, it sure would be swell if you told us.
The Mortician now CLAMPS THE PLIERS around Evan's NIPPLE RING.

MORTICIAN
For what purpose? You seek a back way out of a room with but one door. You can't
cheat Death; there are no escapes.

CLEAR
Bullshit. You told me Death has a distinct design, a blueprint, unalterable. But Alex and
I cheated Death not once, but dozens of times. If the design is flawed, it can be beaten.
A sick smile crosses the Mortician's lips. He yanks the nipple ring
OFF! Kimberly looks on both horrified and awed when Clear doesn't flinch back from
the pliers, where a bloody nub dangles.

MORTICIAN
Such fire in you now. People are always most alive just before they die. Don't you think?
Clear steps back from him, hate flashing in her eyes.

CLEAR
It can be beaten. And you know it.
CREEEAAAK -SLAM! The Mortician rolls Evan's body into the oven.

MORTICIAN
Some say that there is a balance to everything. An equilibrium that is the connective
tissue of the universe. They say that for every lif e there is a death, and for every death
a life...
His words hang in the air. An ominous BREEZE enters.

MORTICIAN
Solus novus anima licet evinco mortis; Only new life can defeat death.
(off their confusion)
The list of life is forever set by the Divine Plan, the guiding hand that plots the course
of the universe, down to its tiniest element s.
Thomas looks to Clear; what's he talking about? The Mortician focuses on Kimberly as
if the others had ceased to exist.

MORTICIAN
The list accounts for every life; from the dawn of man to the great apocalypse. But the
introduction of life that was not meant to be, a soul forbidden to roam the earth, that
could invalidate Death's list, shatter its very existence.
Evan's other eye POPS , startling Thomas and Kimberly.

THOMAS
What the hell does that mean?

MORTICIAN
(with finality)
To figure that out you'll have to follow the sign s.

The Mortician grabs Kimberly.

MORTICIAN
But be warned. To disrupt the grand design is to unravel the tapestry of the universe.
When you pull all the threads apart, you may find yourself hanging from them.
The Mortician finally lets Kimberly go.

CLEAR
One last question. Why is Death working backwards this time?
The Mortician glances at his watch - Evan's bran d new Rolex.

MORTICIAN
(shakes head; a sick smile)
Sorry, time's up.

EXT. GAS STATION - DAY
CLOSE UP - GAS DRIPPING
From the nozzle in Thomas' car. Thomas fills the tank, watching for signs of danger.
Clear's hand is poised over the gas pumps' EMERGENCY

CUT-OFF VALVE
Some SKATE RATS exit the mini -mart with a pack of Camels, followed by
Kimberly, who carries a couple of Red Bulls and hands them out.

THOMAS
New life defeats death? Follow the signs? Where the hell did you find that guy?

KIMBERLY
Yeah, I thought he was supposed to be helpful.

CLEAR
He was. If we can use your ability to see the signs, we can cheat
Death long enough to figure out what "new life" means.
(off their looks)
I know, it worries me that I understand him.
Thomas tops off the tank. Some gas spills to the ground. Quick looks all around sure
enough, one of the Skate Rats is about to strike a match.
CLEAR'S HAND SLAPS the kid in the back of the head, stopping him mid - motion.

CLEAR
What the fuck are you thinking?
The startled Skate Rat shrinks back from Clear's rage.

SKATE RAT
I'm thinkin', suck my junk, bee yatch.
Thomas chuckles to himself and looks at Kimberly who

SMASH CUT TO:
EXT. LAKE - DAY
POV DRIVER. Grease-covered female hands reach out toward a steering wheel of a white van speeding out of control TOWARD A LAKE!
The van crashes through a railing and PLUNGES into the water. In moments, the van fills with water, the driver inside trapped.
Drowning. Horrible.

SMASH CUT TO:
INT. GAS STATION - DAY
KIMBERLY
Comes to Thomas' arms - GASPING uncontrollably for breath. Terror- stricken. She begins hyperventilating.

THOMAS
What is it? What did you see?
It's so bad, Kimberly can't speak. She coughs and gags as if recently drowned. Clear scans the perimeter for immediate dangers.

QUICK CUTS:
A POWER REPAIRMAN
On a cherry picker messes with the transformer, a LAWN BOY pull- starts a WEED WHACKER close to broken glass, a MECHANIC on a tall ladder changes out the gas price numbers, a female DOG WALKER with three dogs approaches the ladder.

CLEAR
You have to tell us now.

KIMBERLY
I...I...
Clear shakes her head by the shoulders and barks commands like an angry drill sergeant.

CLEAR
You're strong. Do you hear me?
You're a fucking warrior. Nothing scares you. In fact you happen to be the single most powerful woman on earth. Now what did you see?
The words slowly take affect. Kimberly becomes centered, getting her breath back, and speaks without a hitch.

KIMBERLY
I was driving a white van. It must've gone out of control because it crashed into a lake and I drowned. It was...horrible.

CLEAR
You were there?

KIMBERLY

I can practically taste the water in my throat. And something else.
The smell of flowers...

CLEAR
(confused)
Then it wasn't just a sign. It was a premonition?
Thomas gently releases her, paces.

THOMAS

Remember the onramp? There was a pregnant woman in a white delivery van.

CLEAR

Holy shit. He said "only new life can defeat death."
(off looks)
If she gives birth to a baby that was never meant to be born, a brand new soul that was never part of
Death's Design...

KIMBERLY

It throws the entire Death list out of whack. And a new list has to be rewritten f rom scratch. We all start over with a clean slate.

THOMAS

It sounds all well and good, but what if we're wrong?

CLEAR

Please, what else could it mean?

KIMBERLY
(to Thomas)
So if you give us the pregnant lady's number, we can warn her about the lake and she'll live long enough to have the baby.

CLEAR

So let's do it.

THOMAS
(realization)
Shit, I don't have her number. She was never interviewed. She took off right after the accident.

KIMBERLY

How are we going to find her?
There must be thousands of white vans in this state.

THOMAS
Hey, I'm a police officer, remember?

INT. A/V ROOM - POLICE STATION - LATER
Thomas works a VCR, scanning BACKWARDS through the video footage from the patrol car camera. We see the SUV's explosive collision with the jack- knifed semi. Kimberly is taken by surprise by the sight of the crash.

KIMBERLY
Oh God...
Thomas sees Kimberly and quickly flicks off the monitor.

THOMAS
I, uh...sorry.
Kimberly notices Clear watching her and toughens up. She forces back the tears and qui ckly wipes the rest away.

KIMBERLY
I know, I know. We need my eyes.
Clear sits beside Kimberly.

CLEAR
It's all right. I'll take watch.
Kimberly looks grateful, and a moment passes between them, but she's already buried the need to cry.

KIMBERLY
I'm okay. Just caught me by surprise. Put it back on.
Clear does, watching the cars seemingly pass in reverse.

CLEAR
Make sure all these people will be at the meeting tonight.

THOMAS
Taken care of.

THE MONITOR
Back, back, back until the Patrol Car slowly creeps backwards down the onramp.

KIMBERLY
There it is.

THOMAS
Got it.

Thomas hits play and we see footage from the patrol car cruising past the White Van. A clean shot of the license plate. Jackpot.
As Thomas slides his chair to a data base and types in the plate number, the pause function dislodges, slowly advancing the tape frame by frame.

CLEAR
I don't get it. Why is everything happening so fast? After Flight
180. A month went by before anyone died. And now five people are dead in less than a day.
Thomas' computer screen finally fills with information.

THOMAS
Here we go. The vehicle's a delivery van registered to Jorge and Isabella Cruz. And Christ, there's almost a dozen domestic disturbance complaints on these two.

CLEAR
We need to hurry.
They all get up and leave.
Ominously, THE MONITOR shows the NEXT VEHICLE creeping behind Nora's Pacer - a white van!

INT. CRUZ HOUSE - NIGHT
Thomas pulls up to an upper-middle class house. Thomas, Kimberly and
Clear get out and start up the unlit path. It's dark, hard to see where they're going, so they negotiate by feeling the bushes aligning the walkway.

THOMAS
Let's lay this on her gently now.
The stress alone could upset the pregnancy.
Kimberly nods, ever creeping closer to the front door when
AUTOMATIC LIGHTS FLASH from over the garage.
All three freeze for a moment, during which we hear STOMPING emanate from within the house, and the lights SHUT OFF.
But nothing else happens. No one comes to a door. Thomas sighs, and as if suddenly remembering his status, he walks fearlessly and purposefully to the front door.
He makes a fist, is about to knock - when the DOOR FLINGS OPEN and a
ROTTWEILER LUNGES for his throat - only to have its collar snagged at the last second by its owner -
JORGE CRUZ, late 30's, handsome, cocky. He speaks above Rotty's

BARKING:
JORGE
What?

THOMAS
I'm Officer Burke. I'm looking for an Isabella Cruz.

Suddenly, with an unexpected fury, Jorge SCREAMS at his dog.

JORGE
Shut up!!!
The Rottweiler cowers, and Jorge shoves it to the floor, where it lands on its feet and fearfully trots away. Jorge's face is once again pleasant, but it's a thin veneer.
Jorge sees Clear and Kimberly behind Thomas and frowns.

THOMAS
Are you Jorge Cruz?

JORGE
Maybe. What's this about?

THOMAS
May we come in?

JORGE
No. What's this about?
ANGLE ON CLEAR - eyeing what appears to be DROPS OF BLOOD on the tile floor.
She takes in what she can see of

THE ROOM
As if a tornado had hit it. Wedding photos smashed and torn.
Furniture over-turned.

THOMAS
(a little stern)
It's about your wife, Isabella.
Now is she here?
Jorge's eyes flicker ever -so- involuntarily behind him.

JORGE
No. I'm alone.
But by now, Thomas has seen everything Clear has and more. He stares through the house, into a bedroom and sees -
A FEMALE FOOT lying half0buried under the bedspr ead.

THOMAS
Look, pal, it's probably nothing.
But I need to see
Jorge is already closing the door.

JORGE
Forget it. You'll need a warrant.
I know, I'm a lawyer.

Clear rushes the door, shoulders it and expertly wriggles past
Jorge's grasp.

JORGE
Stop!!! You can't go in there!!!
Clear tears into the bedroom, grabs the bedspread and THROWS it to the floor to reveal
a YOUNG WOMAN, naked, trembling with fear, takes a closer look at Clear.

YOUNG WOMAN
We never meant to hurt you
Isa...You're not Isabella!
Meanwhile, Jorge yells at Thomas.

JORGE
I'm going to sue your ass!

KIMBERLY
Whose blood is that on the floor?
Defensively, Jorge holds up his arm. Freshly cut.

JORGE
Mine, you idiot. The dog went nuts this afternoon. Now arrest her!

KIMBERLY
Where's Isabella? Did you finally kill her you fucking wife beater?
Jorge flinches. It's time to come clean.

JORGE
We had a fight. Some things got broken, the dog went crazy, she left me. Wouldn't say
where she was going.

THOMAS
What was the fight about?

JORGE
Take a guess.

THOMAS
Does she have a cell phone? A way we can contact her?

JORGE
She did.
He eyes a SHATTERED CELL PHONE on the floor.

CLEAR
We're wasting time with this piece of shit. Let's just get to the meeting.

Jorge turns to soothe the frightened Young Woman in the bed.

JORGE
Hey, when you find her, tell her the kid's half mine.
Clear mutters something as they exit the house.

CLEAR
We can only pray it doesn't come out retarded.
Jorge hisses something at the Rotty, which CHARGES them and SPRINGS!
But Thomas slams the door on the frothing dog just in time.

DISSOLVE TO:
EXT. THOMAS' APARTMENT BUILDING - NIGHT
Rory sits in his Chevette outside an apartment building, staring up at the address. He quickly snorts some powder off his key and wipes his nostrils free of crystals. He takes a breath and exits the car.

INT. THOMAS' APARTMENT BUILDING - NIGHT
Rory follows some PEOPLE into the elevator. The elevator doors close on his shoe trapping Rory in an awkward position.
One MAN frantically pushes the DOORS OPEN button to no avail.
Finally, as the elevator rises, Rory YANKS his foot free.

MAN
Jesus Christ. I wrote to management two weeks ago about these friggin' bumpers.
Rory bends down and inspects his shoe.

RORY
Damn, is that dogshit?
Rory briefly holds the shoe too close to the Man's face - see? - before disgustedly slipping it back on.
DING. The doors open. The man hurries out and the elevator DOORS
CLOSE on Rory's smirking face.

HARD CUT TO:
INT. THOMAS' APARTMENT - LATER
REVEAL - Nora, Rory, and Kat, mortified, sit on a couch. It's obvious the bomb's been dropped, reality has set in. Clear and Kimberly await their reactions. Nora raises a trembling hand.

NORA
Does anybody have a Valium?
Kat opens her purse and hands her a blue pill.

KAT
You'll want to take

Nora pops it in her mouth.

KAT
half of that.
Nora chews, her eyes half dead from bereavement. Across the loft,
Thomas paces, phone in hand.

THOMAS
(quietly, into phone)
Any word yet on the Dodge van?
Damn.
Eugene alone seems unafraid. He uses a GRABBER - a long pole with movable claw
on the end - to OPEN THE SKYLIGHT. When done, he balances the long pole
precariously against the wall.
An OMINOUS BREEZE enters. Clear notices MAGAZINE PAGES blowing over the
desk by the couch.

NORA
So that would mean... I'm next.

EUGENE
Nobody's next. This is crazy.
First death's stalking us and now premonitions?

KAT
This can't be happening. My career's at a peak, I finally met a cute guy, I just bought a
new house...

RORY
Just shut the fuck up and maybe you'll live.
Kat's hands ball into fists. The hatred is mutual. Clear reaches for a nearby cardboard
box on the desk, noticing MAGAZINE PAGES blowing over until their weight tips
over a PENCIL HOLDER which spills pens out. She takes the box to Nora.

CLEAR
You're not next, Nora. Nobody has to be next. That's the point.
Last time, we didn't plan. We weren't organized. Now we can help each other.
She reaches into the box and passes out cell phones to Nora and the others.

CLEAR
Think what would have happened if
Kimberly had been able to warn you with the word pigeons...
Nora's head falls. Kimberly senses her anguish and takes over.

KIMBERLY

The point is, as long as you know what to beware of, you have a fighting chance. It can be beaten.
If I call you and say subway, get to a high rise fast. A place where no subway could possibly go, get it?
Everyone nods in understanding. Rory fidgets, sniffling, then POUNDS the table in frustration. Startling Kat.

RORY
Why the hell did I ever get on
Route 18 in the first place?
That's me, Mr. Dumb Fucking Luck.
Clear, very alert, looks at the tipped PENCIL HOLDER. PENS ROLL toward the end of the desk, toward a large White Pages directory which hangs precariously off the edge just so.

CLEAR
Anyone read today's paper? The article on Evan Shaeffer?
No one says a word.

CLEAR
The only reason he was on Route 18 was because he own the lottery and had to collect the winnings.

RORY
That lucky bastard.

CLEAR
What about the rest of you?
Kimberly, you were driving to
Daytona. Was Route 18 your first choice?

KIMBERLY
The new freeway was faster, but
Route 18 was the way my mom used to take, so...
They take turns going around the room.

THOMAS
Route 18 is Drake's assignment, but he called in sick so I got...
(blanches)
Drake's never sick.

KAT
I was my first day of jury duty.

EUGENE
Jury duty? That's randomly selected by social security numbers.

CLEAR
Random, sure.

EUGENE
What, you think Death planned for each of us to die in the pile up weeks ago? You're nuts.
Clear fumes. Rory looks ill and reaches into his wallet.

RORY
Last July I dialed a wrong number and got a radio station by accident. They asked me what number means "good luck" in Jewish.

KAT
Eighteen. And it's "Hebrew".

RORY
Anyway, I guessed it right and won these.
Rory holds up two Yankee tickets.

RORY
The best way to get to Yankee
Stadium is Route 18.

KIMBERLY
I don't know what's weirder, the dialing a wrong number part or that
Death would set you up nine months in advance.

THOMAS
(realization)
Whoa, nine months?

KIMBERLY
Are you thinking what I'm thinking?

INT. CHEAP MOTEL - NIGHT
ANGLE ON ISABELLA'S PREGNANT BELLY.
REVEAL she's lying down, binging on take- out food, while speaking on the motel phone. A disturbing metallic SQUEAK SCRAPE -SQUEAK can be heard, nearly drowning out the SCREAMING COUPLE next door.

ISABELLA
Yes, I'd like to report a domestic squabble - my name? Isabella Cruz why, does it matter? I'm at the
Super 8 motel. Yes, I own a white van. So what? Just get over here.
Isabella hangs up, recoiling at VIOLENT THUMPS against her wall. PULL

BACK AND UP TO REVEAL the source of the unsettling SQUEAK is a rickety, wobbling CEILING FAN.

INT. THOMAS' APARTMENT - NIGHT
Kimberly whispers into the phone.

KIMBERLY
I'm sorry, Dad, we're having a hard time with Shaina's eulogy. I'll stay here at Virginia's tonight and see you tomorrow. I love you too.
She hangs up, looking guilty for having lied to her father. Clear keeps her eyes on the pens that ROLL on the slightly canted table into the about-to -fall White Pages directory.

CLEAR
Remember everyone, just because
Kimberly's got the power doesn't mean we're not all capable of seeing signs to some extent.
The pens softly tap the phone book one by one until it lazily tips over and PLOPS HEAVILY onto a GOOSE-DOWN THROW PILLOW.
Small feathers from the pillow are carried upwards by the breeze.
Everyone in the room watches them rise.

RORY
It's like Forrest Gump.
They float across the room, ultimately landing on a MOUSETRAP! SNAP!
The trap flies over and knocks into the base of the unstable Grabber
- which tips and slowly slides down the wall.
Clear, in a chair, looks directly above her head at a LARGE SWORDFISH mounted on the wall.
The Grabber picks up speed, arcs downward and hits the mounted
SWORDFISH. The supporting brackets give, causing the SWORDFISH TO TIP and SLIDE DOWNWARD!
Clear lurches back in her chair just in time - the razor sharp bill impales the seat cushion between her legs!

CLEAR
Fuck. Should have seen that coming. The institution's made me soft.
Clear gets up, carefully easing herself around the swordfish. Eugene isn't quite sure what to make of what he's just seen.

EUGENE
If Death has got such a hard-on for you, maybe you should get the hell away from us.

KIMBERLY
We need her. She's the only one who's dealt with this before, idiot!
Kimberly looks self-conscious by her outburst. Clear, however, looks grateful.

CLEAR

We're all going to have to open our eyes from now on. Look out for each other. Sleep in shifts.
(looks around apartment)
And we've got to safeproof this deathtrap.

MONTAGE - SAFEPROOFING THE APARTMENT

Everyone but Nora and Eugene helps unplug appliances, put out the fire, take down hanging objects, switch off the gas, put sharp objects away, affix padding to chart corners...
Kat, placing poisonous cleansers and flammable liquids in a box, nervously pulls out a pack of smokes. Thomas watches as he takes a hanging mirror off the wall.

KAT

Screw this. I'm going outside for a smoke.

THOMAS

You think you should? It's not safe out there.

KAT

So? Nora's gotta bite it before me anyway, right?
Kat steps towards the front door, then remembers the cell phone and grabs it just in case. Thomas smiles 'good job' at her.
Kimberly, unscrewing the light bulb, looks up when Nora rises from the couch in a stupor and struggles to put on her jacket. Kimberly looks concerned.

KIMBERLY

Where are you going, Nora? You okay?
Nora fights the sleeve, dazed and defeated.

NORA

Four years ago my husband died.
Now Tim. There's nothing left for me.
Kimberly stops pouring liquor down the drain.

KIMBERLY

Don't say that. Once you lose hope, it's already too late.
Eugene snickers. Nora looks up, anger surfacing.

NORA

If it's my time to go, to be in heaven with my family, then I can accept that.

KIMBERLY

You can't give up. Don't accept

Death's plan. Trust me, you can fight this. If we can just survive long enough until that baby is born, we can
Nora looks more resolute than ever.

NORA
If you'll excuse me, I have a funeral to prepare.
Everyone looks crushed when Nora heads for the door. Except Eugene, who stands up as well.

EUGENE
Yeah, why am I listening to a girl who just got out of the nut house?
As Eugene heads out, Kimberly becomes enraged and grabs him.

KIMBERLY
Seeing you die once was enough for me.

EUGENE
Whatever. I control my life, not fate.

CLEAR
I'll be sure to put that on your tombstone.
Rory presses a cell phone into Eugene's hand on his way out.

RORY
Be careful. And even if you don't believe, give this to Nora.

INT. THOMAS' APARTMENT BUILDING - NIGHT
Eugene pushes the elevator button a thousand times. Nora nervously ties her long hair back in a single braid.

INT. THOMAS' APARTMENT - CONTINUOUS
The nervous group finishes safe-proofing the apartment.
RORY, standing on the couch, pulls a POLICE ACADEMY DIPLOMA off the wall - and slips - stumbling BACKWARDS into the closet.
Staggering, he accidentally knocks some COAT HANGARS and a VOLLEYBALL TROPHY from the high shelf to the floor.
Thomas whips around and sees that Rory's not hurt. He then lowers his gaze and sees
The figurine of a VOLLEYBALL TROPHY is framed by a tangled jumble of wire COAT HANGARS. Suddenly, STREETLIGHT FLICKERS ON for the evening.
Oddly, it only illuminates the Trophy/Hangar array.
From Rory's vantage point, it looks like a surreal sculpture of a man with hooks emanating from his body. The sodium vapor lamp casts an
OMINOUS GLOW around the image.

RORY
...man with hooks. I see a man with hooks. Someone?!?!

The others look over, trying to see what he does.

THOMAS
(unsure)
I kinda see it, yeah. So...Nora's going to be killed by a man with hooks?
Kimberly and Clear stare at the volleyball trophy - the street lamp ominously FLICKERS OUT AND DIES.
Everyone looks around for a hesitant beat, then Thomas picks up his cell phone. Clear first walks, then RUNS out the door.

INT. THOMAS' APARTMENT BUILDING - CONTINUOUS
The elevator finally comes. Eugene and Nora get inside, standing in front of a gaunt looking man holding a cardboard box full of

PROSTHETIC LIMBS.
MUZAK plays AC/DC's HIGHWAY TO HELL.

EUGENE
Going down, right?
The Gaunt Man says nothing. The DOORS CLOSE.

INT. ELEVATOR - CONTINUOUS
Eugene stares blankly at the CONCAVE MIRROR in the upper corner. He's disturbed by the WARPED REFLECTION OF:
THE GAUNT MAN leans closer to Nora's hair and as the doors finally close, he leans over and SMELLS it. Creepy.

EUGENE
Um, by the way, your shoe's untied.
Nora bends down to tie her shoelace (the one that snapped). She tries tying the long dangling shoelace to the stubby one as Eugene's cell phone VIBRATES in his hand. Startled, he drops it to the floor. Then looks embarrassed.

EUGENE
Probably for you, anyway.
Nora picks it up. STATIC CRACKLES. It's hard to make out Thomas' yelling.

NORA
Officer Burke? I can't hear...
A beat of confusion, then she slowly turns to see the clawed hooks and hands of the Prosthetic limbs. Terror. She freezes.

EUGENE
What is it? What's wrong?
But Nora's too frightened to speak. Eugene grabs the phone, hearing unintelligible STATIC.

INTERCUT CLEAR
As she frantically hits the elevator button. When it fails to come, she runs downstairs.

INT. ELEVATOR - CONTINUOUS
Nora slowly rises to her feet, feverishly mouthing a prayer... As the door opens, Nora rushes out - unseen to her, her long braid gets snagged on one of the PROSTHETIC HOOKS, YANKING her backwards.

NORA
Let me go let me go!

EUGENE
Oh, watch it, you've caught your uh...
The Guant Man's sweet voice and demeanor are a clear contrast to his outward appearance.

MAN
Goodness gracious, darling, let me help you with...
Nora panic,s as Eugene and the Man try to untangle her braid. Nora desperately spins her body around, sticking her head back inside the elevator.
Kat appears in the lobby, smoking a cigarette.

KAT
You alright, Nora?
The elevator DOORS begin to close, and CLAMP around Nora's neck, her head inside, body outside the elevator.
Eugene pounds on the BUMPERS, but they don't seem to work!

NORA
My God, someone please let me out of this

INTERCUT
The UP BUTTON is lit. Clear rushes to the lobby.
The Elevator RISES!
INSIDE THE ELEVATOR, Eugene watches Nora's head drop to floor level - then he pounds the Emergency Button - which SHORTS OUT!
Nora's body lifts upwards from the force of the elevator floor!
Nora's screams of terror and agony fill the air as the elevator repeatedly LURCHES UPWARDS.
Kat gasps in horror to see this poor woman suspended above the floor.
It lurches. And lurches. And lurches. The horror never ends.
Clear comes from the stairwell and is shocked by the sight. She runs to the elevator doors, trying to pry them apart to no avail.
All Kat can do, crying, is grab hold of Nora's flailing legs and try to pull her back down.

The elevator lurches a final time. NORA'S HEADLESS BODY fall down into Kat's arms, knocking her to the floor. Kat freaks, skittering away as the body convulses.

INSIDE THE ELEVATOR
Eugene balls his hands to his mouth in undeniable fear. A bloodcurdling moan escapes him. He stares transfixed as Nora's head, still aghast in terror, rolls around the floor. The sight clearly sends Eugene over the edge. He SCREAMS, CLAWS AND POUNDS, desperate to escape the elevator.

INT. THOMAS' APARTMENT - MOMENTS LATER
Eugene suddenly bursts through the door, babbling incoherently. Kimberly, Thomas and Rory look on, bewildered.

EUGENE
...no escapes my ass. I control my fate. I die on my terms, hear me Reaper cockscuker?!
Eugene's in another world. He approaches Thomas and lunges for his GUN - yanking it from the holster!

THOMAS
What the hell are you...?

EUGENE
Ain't going out like that. On my terms!

THOMAS
Just take it easy!
A twisted insane smile comes to Eugene's face as he jams the gunbarrel to his temple. The others shrink back in terror.
He PULLS THE TRIGGER. CLICK! Eugene tries again. CLICK!
Thomas looks stunned as Eugene goes through every round, CLICK CLICK

CLICK CLICK CLICK CLI CK...
Kimberly breaths a sigh of relief.

KIMBERLY
You don't keep it loaded?
Thomas' eyes disagree. He reaches in and GRABS the gun away from Eugene, who stands there trembling. Thomas cracks open the cylinder.
Loaded.

RORY
Maybe they were all duds.

THOMAS
Six in a row? Never. Impossible.

That's like
(sinking realization)
...winning the lottery.

CLEAR (O.S.)
It wasn't his turn to die.
Everyone turns to see Clear and Kat, standing in the doorway,
DRENCHED IN BLOOD. Kat trembles uncontrollably.

KAT
Can we find the pregnant woman, please?

DISSOLVE TO:
INT. THOMAS' APARTMENT - DAWN
Flashing lights from rescue vehicles illuminate the living room. In the newly conformed
safe house, Kat and Clear relax as best they can in Thomas' dry clothes.
Thomas makes another phone call. In the corner, Eugene shivers to himself. Desperately
looking for signs of danger. He looks over to
Clear.

EUGENE
Um, Clear? I'm sorry...about before. I...

CLEAR
Your entire world view just went out the window. I couldn't expect a religious
conversation overnight.
We'll get through this.
(beat)
I promise.
Eugene looks immensely relieved. Rory ambles over to Kimberly, his typical
callousness gone.

RORY
Can I ask you a question?

KIMBERLY
Sure.

RORY
When I die. Is it gonna hurt?

KIMBERLY
I...I don't know.
Rory nods. He expected as much. He fishes his LICENSE and KEYS out of his pocket.

RORY

And you're gonna die after me, right?

KIMBERLY
I guess so.

RORY
(re: keys and license)
Would you take these? And if I die...
(tears well up)
Could you throw all my drugs out?
Paraphernalia, porno, you know...
Anything that would break my mom's heart.
Kimberly looks deeply into his eyes, looking for the punchline. When she doesn't see one, she nods tenderly and takes the keys.
The PHONE RINGS. Rory jumps at the sound, paranoid eyes in scan mode.
Thomas answers, speaks softly, hangs up.

THOMAS
A one very pissed off Ms. Isabella
Cruz is being detained up in
Greenwood. Let's finish this thing.

EXT. COUNTRY ROADS - DAY
Kat's Ford Expedition winds its way through rural New York.
A SPORTS CAR speeds past on the left, then as it pulls in front of the Exped ition, its slipstream sucks over some debris from the shoulder; a thin metal piece of trim, which bounces in front of Kat's
Expedition's left front tire.
CU KAT'S WHEEL WELL the metal trim is shot upward into the wheel well, where it lodges firmly, its sharp metal edge GRINDING AGAINST

THE RUBBER.
INSIDE THE CAR
Kat drives, Thomas reading directions in the shotgun seat. Kimberly,
Eugene and Rory ride in back. In the CARGO area, Clear scans out the rear window for danger.
Rory fidgets.

RORY
Is this safe, guys? I mean, someone in this car is about to get whacked. Do the rest of us really feel like sitting next to him?
(off Kat's glare)
Or her. Hopefully her.
An uncomfortable beat.

THOMAS

Guys, let's not panic. Isabella's safe.

KIMBERLY
How do you know?

THOMAS
You said she was going to drive into a lake. How can she when she's in protective custody?

INT. SHERIFF'S STATION - DAY
Isabella, pissed, is in a holding tank. Small town deputy STEVE ADAMS, 30's, CLEANS HIS GUN in her direction.

ISABELLA
What do you mean "grand theft auto?" This is insane.

STEVE
Hopefully the district judge can straighten it all out by Monday mor ning.

ISABELLA
(figures it out)
Jorge. When I get out of here I'm going to sue his cheating ass off.
As she fumes, a rivulet of WATER streaks down her leg.

IS ABELLA
Oh my God.
Steve, at first confused, sees the water and gasps.

STEVE
Are you kidding me?! Oh, man.
He rushes across the room, pulls a lever, unlocking the cell.

STEVE
C'mon. Let's go.
As Steve throws on his jacket, we reveal its prominent emblem:

GREENWOOD LAKE SHERIFF DEPARTMENT.
EXT. SHERIFF'S STATION - MOMENTS LATER
Small town station. Only one patrol car. In the patrol car, Isabella buckles up in the sho tgun seat, the belt stretched tightly across her belly.
Deputy Steve tries the ignition, but the car won't start.

STEVE
Damn, they always stick me with the clunker.

ISABELLA

Take my van!

EXT. WESTCHESTER COUNTY - DAY
KAT'S EXPEDITION speeds through a yellow light and continues on.

CLOSE ON EXPEDITION'S LEFT TIRE
Metal sheers away more rubber.

INSIDE THE EXPEDITION
Rory, antsy, rubbing his nostrils, stares at two Yankee tickets.

RORY
Here's what I don't get. For nine months, Death does all this shit to make sure I win these tickets and end up on Route 18 at exactly the right time for the pile up...

KAT
Yeah?

RORY
But why single me out? What am I in the great scheme of things?
You'd think I stepped off Flight
180 or something... Fucking weird, man.

THOMAS
You want weird? Last year, my partner and I were heading out for the graveyard shift.
A call comes in about a train wreck and Frank decides to let me handle it alone.
(beat)
Frank died that night in a shootout. I'd be dead too if that call had come in just ten seconds later.
Everyone nods in that 'life's weird' reverence kind of way.

KAT
I got that beat. So like, last
May, I was supposed to stay at this cheesy bed and breakfast in
Pennsylvania. There was a major gas leak no one knew about and all the guests suffocated during the night.

RORY
Yeah, so what happened?

KAT
I never mad it. The Greyhound bus
I was on splattered some chick all over the road and we had to stop.

CLEAR
Was that in Mt. Abraham?

KAT
Yeah. How did you know?

CLEAR
(sinking realization)
That bus you were on? It killed
Terry Mathers. She was supposed to die on Flight 180.

KAT
I'm not sure I

THOMAS
Shit. The call about the train wreck that saved my life? That was the night I scraped up Billy
Hitchcock.

RORY
Who?

KIMBERLY
Another kid from Flight 180.
A chill passes over the group.

INT. WINDING ROADS - DAY
Deputy Steve speeds the White Van up the narrow winding road.
Isabella breathes Lamaze- style through intense pain.

ISABELLA
Promise me...I won't have the baby...in this van.
Speeding up the incline, Steve tries to speed around a Volkswagon
Beetle, but cars scream by in the opposite direction.

ISABELLA
Get around it!!!
Steve leans on the horn and stomps the gas, dangerously riding the shoulder around the Beetle.
Way ahead of the Beetle, on the left side, is a LAKE.

EXT. WINDING ROADS
BRIAN GIBBONS, 15, cheerfully drives a TRACTOR hauling a WHOODCHIPPER across the high crest of the empty road toward a pile of thick branches.
The Tractor unexpectedly stalls in the middle of the road. He tries the ignition, pumps the gas. Nothing...
Only by standing on the tractor can Brian see the White Van speeding up the hill toward him. He jumps down and frantically tires starting the tractor. Once, twice, nothing.

EXT. KAT'S EXPEDITION - CONTINUOUS
CU FRONT TIRE - METAL shreds away more rubber.

INT. KAT'S EXPEDITION - CONTINUOUS
Rory excitedly makes a connection.

RORY
Remember the theater in Paris that collapsed last year, killed everyone inside?
Everyone nods, anticipating...

RORY
I had tickets to go, but one day
I'm in Paris, trippin' on acid, sippin' lattes an' such, and this dude gets whacked by a
falling sign.

CLEAR
Carter.

RORY
Freaked me out so bad I hid in a shopping cart for four hours.
'Course, missed the show...

CLEAR
What about you, Kimberly? Did you anyone from Flight- ?
Clear stops when she sees all the color has drained from Kimberly's face. Even Eugene
looks concerned.

EUGENE
Are you okay?
The car becomes completely silent (except for the slight SCRAPING) as
Kimberly prepares to tell her story.

KIMBERLY
A little over a year ago, my mother and I went to the mall. I was supposed to meet her
outside, but I got caught up watching some news report about some kid who committed
suicide. I kept thinking, "How can you strangle yourself in a bathtub?" That's retarded.
Thomas mouths, "Tod?" to Clear. Clear nods.

KIMBERLY
It felt wrong. And yet...
(continuing)
There were gunshots outside and I ran...
(chokes up)
Some kids tried to jack her car.
She fought them off - she was a fighter - and they killed her.

Kimberly looks to Clear.

KIMBERLY
After the funeral I had this overwhelming feeling that it should have been me. I figured
that's how everyone must feel. But I guess I was right.
Thomas reaches between the seats and takes Kimberly's hand. As he looks into her eyes,
Kat takes her own eyes off the road to light a cigarette.

INTERCUT BRIAN
The tractor is safely off the road next to a wood pile. Brian grabs a cord and starts up
the whoodchipper.

INT. KAT'S EXPEDITION - CONTINUOUS
CLEAR
It's all starting to come together.
When Alex got us off Flight 180, it didn't just change our lives. It affected everyone and
everything we've come into contact with ever since.

EUGENE
I'm not sure I understand.

CLEAR
Being alive after our time caused an outward ripple - a rift in
Death's design.
Eugene nods, slowly getting it.

EUGENE
So if you never got off the plane, none of us would be ali ve in the first place.

CLEAR
That's why Death is working backwards. It's tying up all the loose ends, sealing the rift
once and for all �
This chapter of the screenplay contains scene(s) that do not appear or occur elsewhere
in the final movie. In order to maintain the integrity of the screenplay, it has not been
edited.

CU LEFT TIRE
A thick retread sheers itself onto the pavement.

BRIAN
The wood chipper roar s loudly. Suddenly, some forgotten stray chunk
SHOOTS from the spout
The airborne chunk of WOOD CRACKS the White Van's windshield. Steve veers out
of control.
Kat sees the White Van ahead swerving into HER LANE. She quickly jerks the wheel
to the right.

Kat's LEFT FRONT TIRE BLOWS! It sends rubber flying and the entire
SUV pulls hard to the left, spinning her out of control into the oncoming lane of traffic
- toward the White Van!
Isabella SCREAMS! Steve jerks the wheel to the left! The White Van has a close near
miss with the Expedition, and goes off the road toward a LAKE!

STEVE
Hang on!
The SUV misses the tractor but sails off the other side of the embankment, spinning and
rolling towards

THE GIBBONS' FARM
At the bottom of the hill of a large rural farm, a PROPANE TANK sits at the edge of
the property!
The SUV barrels down the hill - coming right for it!

INSIDE THE SUV
All Kat can do is cover her head with her arms.

THE WHITE VAN
Speeding toward the lake! Isabella SCREAMS, in pain, not fear. The
White Van is ready for splashdown.
Steve finesses the hand brake while tapping the accelerator. He's able to right the van
away from the water without so much as a hard jerk.

STEVE
We're okay, we're okay.

THE PROPANE TANK
It's about to get creamed - but the bouncing Expedition just barely misses it! It
continues, backwards, CRASHING through a temporary fence and right into

AN AGRICULTURAL CONSTRUCTION SITE!
The Expedition plows past earth movers, crashing through irrigation ditches and pipes,
shrapnel flying everywhere.
Just as the Expedition comes to a stop, an IRRIGATION PIPE ROCKETS through the
rear window miraculously missing Clear and Rory coming to a rest just behind Kat's
head.

INSIDE THE WHITE VAN
Steve sees the wreckage on the other side of the highway and slows down. Isabella
squeezes his hand white.

ISABELLA
Please. It's not going to wait.

STEVE
I've got to stop and help those people.

ISABELLA
Do you want to deliver this baby?
Steve looks ill, then sees another car stopping by the crash. He floors it and speaks into the shoulder mic of his cop radio.

THE EXPEDITION
The dust settles in the silent car. The only sound is a QUIET, WET
WHEEZE. Clear, dazed, looks around carefully, avoiding the METAL
SPIKE that skewers the vehicle.
Rory holds his trembling hand before his eyes as if amazed to see it.
Kimberly shakes her hair, spilling glass onto the floor. Kat tries to open the door, but it won't budge.

KAT
Not my time. Amazing...

THOMAS
Is everybody alright?

A BLOODY HAND SEIZES HIS SHOULDER!
Thomas turns to see
Eugene SPASMING in the back seat! He clutches his ribcage in agony and wheezes!
Blood trickles from his mouth.

KAT
He can't breathe! He can't breathe!

CLEAR
Oh my god, Eugene!?
Eugene's head tilts forward, unconscious.

EXT. GIBBONS' FARM - DAY
BRIAN GIBBONS jumps off the tractor and sprints down the hill toward the accident.
At the edge of the property is a common farm FENCE made from wooden posts bridged by two thick wires.
Brian skillfully climbs between the wires and runs past a DEAD OAK
TREE ten feet inside the fence. In the BG, MR. GIBBONS darts inside a double-wide construction trailer.

MR. GIBBONS (O.S.)
Call 9- 1-1!

WE FOLLOW BRIAN

To the crash site. Brian's jaw drops as he absorbs the chilling sight of a guy and a girl dragging a blood- soaked man from the back seat to perform CPR on him.
Around Brian, voices mesh in a surreal haze.

THOMAS
Stop it, don't move him!

KIMBERLY
He can't breathe damn it. I think his lung's collapsed!

CLEAR
Someone call for help!
We STEADICAM around Brian to reveal a woman screaming from the driver's seat. The sound is surreal.

KAT
I can't move my fucking leg!
Please get me out of here before it explodes!
The color drains from Brian's face as the dying man on the ground coughs blood and the girl performing CPR recoils.
The moment is still surreal as Brian steps back, further away from the horrors he can't face. Into the street
And Rory yanks him back from imminent death as an AMBULANCE SPEEDS onto the property.

RORY
Watch it, dude!
That SNAPS Brian back to reality. Sounds become normal again. Brian collects himself and SNIFFS the air. He then drops to ground level, looking under the Expedition for something.

KIMBERLY
Help us, we need help over here!

BRIAN
(to Kat, reassuringly)
I don't smell any gas. And none's dripping, either.
Brian sticks his head in Kat's window and peers down at her trapped leg. He swipes the broken glass away from the window with this thick flannel sleeve, reaches in, and tries to YANK the door open with all his might.
No good, Kat SCREAMS in pain.

KAT
Stop that! I still need this foot, thank you.
Brian steps back as the emergency vehicle speeds over.

DISSOLVE TO:
EXT. GIBBON'S FARM - LATER
Clear watches two EMTS lo ad Eugene into the back of an ambulance. An oxygen mask
has been placed over his mouth.

CLEAR
Be careful with that, check the gages on the regulator and be mindful of overdoses. Oh,
watch for potholes and puddles.
As Clear continues, the exasperated Paramedics do their best to ignore her. When she
tries to climb inside, she is pushed away.

CLEAR
Look, I made him a promise

PARAMEDIC
Sorry. There's no room.
Again, she's shoved away and steps back, helpless.
Thomas and Kimberly stand by Kat, still trapped in the SUV.

THOMAS
Get that over here! Move move move!
A RESCUE WORKER carries the JAWS of LIFE past Clear towards the
Expedition.

RESCUE WORKER
Excuse me, hot soup coming through.
The hydraulic hose that leads back to the Power Unite WRAPS AROUND

CLEAR'S LEG.
As the hose tightens, Clear realizes she's surrounded by shards of glass and metal. She
quickly WRESTLES herself free of the hose and watches the Paramedics lock Eugene's
gurney into place.

CLEAR
One more thing. Watch out for power lines.
The doors slam, revealing the PHELPS MEMORIAL HOSPITAL logo. The ambulance
speeds off, spraying gravel at her.
She reaches into her pocket and withdraws a CRUSHED cell phone. Shit.
She runs back over to Thomas.

CLEAR
We have to contact Isabella now!
A NEWS VAN tries to weave through the emergency vehicles to get closer to teh
accident.

ANGLE ON NEWS VAN UNDERCARRIAGE

It sinks into the loose dirt, SCRAPING A LARGE ROCK. The gas tank

PUNCTURES.
EMT'S angrily wave the news van back to the road, where it parks near the twin wire fence opposite the DEAD OAK TREE.
Immediately, A CAMERA CREW exits the van to catch the action. Rory steps behind the News Van, making sure he can't be seen, and digs into his sock, coming up with a bindle. A SMILE...

THOMAS (O.S.)
Rory!!!
Rory cringes at his name, pockets his stash, then EXITS FRAME. WE
PUSH IN, the news van gas tank is leaking. A SMALL DRIP...

EXT. GIBBON'S FARM - CONTINUOUS
Thomas, Kimberly, Clear and Rory watch the JAWS OF LIFE being clamped onto Kat's door.

THOMAS
Where's the cell phone Clear gave you?

RORY
I dunno. I think I gave it to
Eugene back at your place.

THOMAS
Damn it. We have to call the
Greenwood Police Station and warn
Isabella.
Thomas runs in the direction of some local POLICE. After he leaves,
Rory drifts away from the pack, hand in pocket.
Kimberly moves back to Kat, who chain -smokes in the front seat of the
Expedition.

KIMBERLY
You doing alright in there?

KAT
My legs are starting to cramp up.
And God, why am I so thirsty? Does anyone have any Fiji?
The KA-CHUNK of the Jaws of Life next to Kat startles her half to death.

KAT
Christ, you wanna give me a heads up next time, pal?
Brian and Mr. Gibbons approach with a cup of tap water. They hand it to kat, who frowns but drinks anyway.

CUT TO:
THE DRIP
Of the leaking gas becomes a steady trickle. GAS SLITHERS over packed dirt, around debris, toward the crash site.

BACK TO:
THOMAS DARK ROOM
Speaks to another COP who clicks off his radio.

COP
She's at Phelps Memorial. They're prepping her to give birth right now.

THOMAS
Where's that?

COP
A few miles up the road. Near the docks.

KAT
Lights one cigarette off the other KA -CHUCNK! The sound makes her flinch, dropping the cigarette on the floor.

KAT
Damn, can't you be quieter with that thing?

RESCUE WORKER
(dripping scorn)
Sure, I'll just set it to the
"quiet" mode.
Kat rescues the glowing cigarette from around her feet and inhales.
KA-CHUNK!!! She jumps again, but maintains her composure.

MEANWHILE
The gasoline purposefully trickles down corrugated steel, through pipes, closer and closer to the Expedition. At one point, the gas even disappears into a hole in the ground, only to resurface twenty feet closer to the site...

KIMBERLY
Looks confused to watch Rory climb between the fence wires and drift the Dead Oak Tree into the field. Thomas runs down the hill toward
Kimberly.

THOMAS
We gotta go now. Isabella's in labor.
Rescue Workers pull off a large chunk of door. KA-CHUNK! Kat

Flinches.

KIMBERLY
What about that?

CLEAR
(calls over to Kat)
How you doing in there, hero?

KAT
(re: spike behind head)
I guess it could be worse.
Brian hands out drinks to Rescue Workers.

THOMAS
So let's go...Where the hell is
Rory?!
Thomas sees Rory in the field and angrily hops the fence, heading directly under the dead Oak Tree.
Rory, his back to everyone, finally opens the BINDLE. Enraptured, he delicately unfolds it...

KIMBERLY
Is put on alert by a fresh BREEZE. Her attention is caught by the
WINDOW of an emergency vehicle. IN THE REFLECTION, Kimberly sees a man sitting on the Expedition, but when she spins ar ound, there's no one there.
KA-CHUNG! The door comes off the Expedition, finally freeing Kat!
Everyone applauds!

KIMBERLY
Wait!
Mr. Gibbons, applauding with everyone else, chooses that very moment to sit on the bumper.

DEPLOYING THE AIRBAG!
SLAMMING Kat's head backwards through the spike, HEAD-KABOB.
Kat's dead limp hand drops her last cigarette which bounces along the hard dirt toward the oncoming gas. Closer, closer,.. The
BREEZE KICKS UP, aiding the cigarette.
WHOOSH, the gas fuse catches. The blusih flame travels through pipes, over rocks, racing toward the news VAN.
Kimberly , half-traumatized, watches an ominous BREEZE rustle through the field, up to the trees, toward Thomas.
The GAS BURNS up an incline, and disappears into the ground... And pops up twenty feet closer to the News Van.

Kimberly follows the BREEZE to the dead oak tree under which Thomas stands. And blows a large branch until it snaps! A startled Thomas sees it fall just in time to DIVE to safety.

Clear, seeing the flame, instinctively runs from the van.

CLEAR
Get back!

BOOM! The news van's explosion hurls two fence posts just over

Thomas' head, end over end, the two lengths of wire stretched between them. The flying garrote heads directly for

Rory, who sorts hard, stands up with a satisfied smile - and is sliced into three sharp cuts of beef.

The silence from the emergency crew is deafening. Mr. Gibbons starts crying hysterically.

MR. GIBBONS
I didn't mean to do it - I didn't know.

Kimberly numbly stares at the fallen branch, the one that caused

Thomas to step out of the path of the flying fence.

KIMBERLY
(to herself)
It wasn't his turn. And it's not my turn.

Kimberly sees the corpses of Kat and Rory, buries the pain, and approaches Mr. Gibbons.

KIMBERLY
Give me the keys to your truck.
Now!

MR. GIBBONS
(hysterical)
Anything you want. Anything. I wish I knew. I didn't...

Mr. Gibbons hands Kimberly the keys.

EXT. WESTCHESTER COUNTY - MOMENTS LATER
Kimberly drives Thomas and Clear in the Gibbons' truck. All are numb.

THOMAS
(buckling up)
Hurry up. There's no time. She's about to give birth.

Kimberly unbuckles her seatbelt and floors it.

CLEAR
What are you doing? You're going to kill us!

KIMBERLY
No. If anyone dies from a crash now, it'll be me. But I can't die if Eugene and Isabella are still alive. I'm last on Death's list.

CLEAR
Are you crazy? What makes you think you'd survive?

KIMBERLY
What happened when Eugene tried to kill himself out of turn?

CLEAR
(considering)
Six duds in a row.

KIMBERLY
And when it was Rory's turn to die, and Thomas was in the way?

THOMAS
That branch fell and saved my life.
You're right, Death's maintaining the order.

KIMBERLY
Let's pray that Isabella's still alive.
The truck speeds into the horizon.

EXT. PHELP'S MEMORIAL HOSPITAL - ESTABLISHING SHOT
INT. DELIVERY ROOM - DAY
Typical chatter as the staff preps Isabella. Steve paces nervously in the background.

STAFF
...contractions coming quicker now.
Take her pressure and CTG. One centimeter dilation. Prep the epidural stat.
Isabella breathes Lamaze style in the hospital bed, her feet in stirrups. A NURSE rocks Isabella's body back and forth, until her back arches almost unnaturally forward.
In the BG, an OBSTETRICIAN, 50s, sterilizes his hands in a scrub sink.
A female ANESTHESIOLOGIST hustles over, swabbing a LONG EPIDURAL NEEDLE. The nurse places a mask over Isabella's face. The Anesthesiologist lowers the needle to the base of Isabella's spine.

ANESTHESIOLOGIST
She's going to have to stop moving if I'm going to
The Nurse SNEEZES.

ANESTHESIOLOGIST
Goddamn it, keep her still!

NURSE
Sorry, doctor.

XCU NEEDLE
Tracing skin between Isabella's constantly moving vertebra.

ANGLE ON BUMBLEBEE
It buzzes about the room, darting between the he ads of the doctors and nurses, hovering above the
ANESTHESIOLOGIST, who traces the long needle down Isabella's spine, finding the proper vertebrae.

ANESTHESIOLOGIST
Perfectly still now...
Everyone freezes. SILENCE. As the tip of the needle presses the skin down
The BEE lands on the Anesthesiologist's ear. And STINGS!

FLINCH!
The NEEDLE SINKS IN - a NURSE GASPS. Did something go wrong?

ANESTHESIOLOGIST
Done.
(tears welling)
Now could someone please find the open window and fucking close it?

EXT. SUBURBAN STREET - CONTINUOUS
Kimberly speeds the truck down some dangerously twisty roads slick from wet leaves.

KIMBERLY
This makes no sense. Isabella was supposed to crash her van into a lake. Could we have altered her destiny when we had her arrested?

CLEAR
I don't think so. Alex's premonitions happened exactly as he saw them no matter how much we tried to change it.

THOMAS
Then the only way to survive is to get to the hospital and protect
Eugene and Isabella for as long as we can.

CLEAR
If only Alex and I had done that with the others, Alex might still be...
A somber beat. Then Thomas looks over at the speedometer.

THOMAS
Um, Kimberly? This is a neighborhood. You may wanna slow it down.

KIMBERLY
Don't worry. Nothing can happen to us.

THOMAS
I wasn't worried about us.
Suddenly, Kimberly clutches her throat!

HARD CUT TO:
INT. HOSPITAL ROOM - DAY
UNKNOWN POV
A NURSE hovers over us in a hospital, WRESTLING us down by the look of things. There is SCREAMING all around. The image comes at us so fast, we see only the briefest glimpse of the NAMETAG on her uniform:

KALARJIAN
THOMAS (O.S.)
Kimberly! Slow down!

BACK TO:
INT. TRUCK - CONTINUOUS
Kimberly "comes to" at the wheel FLAILING DESPERATELY at the steering wheel. She even claws at Thomas who tries to control the neglected steering wheel.

CLEAR
Slow down! We're...
Kimberly looks up as the truck comes around a blind curve, where cars are backed up at a stop sign. Kimberly screams and SLAMS on the brakes.
The truck SKIDS on wet leaves, completely out of control, towards a LANDSCAPING TRUCK parked on the shoulder.
Kimberly's truck hits the loading ramps and launches itself twenty feet into the air, DUKES OF HAZZARD-style.
And lands miraculously without a scratch! On a parallel road. And keeps going. Dumb, insane fucking luck.
Kimberly shakes off her premonition and looks out the rear window.
She turns around with a cocky smile.
She rubs her throat and FLOORS IT again to Thomas' horror, more determined.

CLEAR
(eyes darting)
What did you see? What am I looking for?

KIMBERLY
No, it's not here. This one was different. More like the pile up and the van going into the lake.
It wasn't just a sign, I was there.

CLEAR
(confused)
Another premonition?

KIMBERLY
Yes. I was in a hospital. There was screaming... A nurse was choking me. I couldn't tell wh at she looked like, but the name tag was right in my face. Kalarjian.

THOMAS
Kalarjian?

KIMBERLY
I think a nurse named Kalarjian is going to choke Isabella to death!

INT. PRIVATE ROOM - DAY
WIPING FRAME, a NURSE enters a room and reads a clipboard on an unseen patient's bed.
REVEAL EUGENE lying in a hospital bed, wired to the latest medical hardware. Nearby, a RESPIRATOR plunges up and do wn, the RESPIRATOR
TUBE snaking down Eugene's throat.
The NURSE'S HAND reaches down to Eugene's neck...
Eugene WINCES when the Nurse gives the tube a friendly little SHAKE to check if it's stable.

NURSE
Sorry. Can you feel that in your trachea?
Eugene rolls his eyes. Stupid question.

NURSE
Quite complaining. I got burnt babies in the Children's Ward braver than you.
She sticks an electri c thermometer in his ear. Eugene opens his mouth as if to speak.

NURSE
Don't bother. You won't be talking for at least a month. Think you can handle that, Jabberjaw?
Eugene looks ready to cry. The Nurse sits on the bed, jarring Eugene enough to make him WINCE again.

NURSE
Don't worry. Everyone learns to love me once they get used to my sense of humor, okay?
Eugene looks grat eful to see a humane side to this creature.

EXT. WINDY ROADS - DAY

The pick up truck races to the hospital. As Kimberly speeds past a billboard, a POLICE CAR pulls in hot pursuit.

KIMBERLY
Shouldn't we pull over?

THOMAS
No time. Keep going. I wouldn't know how to explain any of this anyway.
At the next intersection, TWO MORE COP CARS APPEAR.

KIMBERLY
Oh come on.
The pick up truck blows by the second pair of cop cars, which instantly join the high speed chase. Kimberly takes a long look in the rearview mirror at the TAILGATING COPS. She then inspects the road ahead.

UP IN THE DISTANCE
A busy six-lane intersection.

KIMBERLY
What do you want me to do?

CLEAR
(hesitated beat)
Speed up.

KIMBERLY
Yeah, fuck 'em.
(to Thomas)
No offense.
Kimberly SPEEDS toward the intersection. She pulls her seatbelt aside, making sure it offers ZERO protection. Thomas jumps in the backseat, buckles up...

CLEAR
Be alive, Isabella, please be alive.
Kimberly's eyes widen in fear. Her foot hesitates over the brake pedal as
The truck blindly blazes through the busy intersection, miraculously missing every car!
The police are just barely able to fishtail into 90 degree turns, avoiding the intersection completely.
Kimberly's eyes open and she lets out a victory cry.

INT. PRIVATE ROOM - DAY
ANGLE ON
Oxygen valve. PAN OVER AND DOWN TO
Eugene tries to watch a news flash of HIS accident on the TV across the room, but a bulky ORDERLY blocks his view.

ANCHOR MAN (O.S.)
...ironically impaled through the head as a result of an emergency airbag deploying.
As Eugene shudders with dread, the Orderly pushes a huge cart in front of him, again
obscuring his view. Eugene frantically pantomimes writing.

ORDERLY
Need a pen? Sure. If you like,
I'll bring crosswords for you, too.
Eugene tries nodding his thanks, but the tube in his throat hampers his movement.

ANCHOR WOMAN (O.S.)
...police Have speculated that one of the deaths may have been narcotics related and
urge children to stay away from d rugs.
Finally, the Orderly pushes the cart away, revealing the TV. An
ANCHOR MAN taps his pages on the desktop.

ANCHOR MAN
Good advice, Sue. And stay in school. Up next, Johnny Showers has the weather...
A WEATHERMAN dressed as a frog points out cloud formations.
Eugene, tormented, stares at the screen as the Orderly begins pushing the huge cart out
of the room.
The sound of a SKIDDING CAR fills the room. It comes from the TV which shows a
PSA featuring CRASH TEST DUMMIES.

ORDERLY
Jeez, it's freezing in here.
The Orderly flicks the thermostat and one by one, VENTS CLOSE just below the
ceiling.
Eugene's eyes fill with terror - he knows something's wrong.

ANGLE ON OXYGEN HOSE -
Bursting. It HISSES softly. We follow the OBLIVIOUS ORDERLY out of the room.

INT. HOSPITAL CORRIDOR - CONTINUOUS
A hospital ADMINISTRATOR briskly strides up to the Orderly.

ADMINISTRATOR
What are you doing? The Henzels are still waiting for you in the
Children's Ward
The Orderly smacks his forehead - shit. Totally forgot.

ORDERLY
Right, right, right. Gregory's big day.

ADMINISTRATOR

And Mrs. Dempsey in hydrotherapy can't feel her legs.
The Orderly, nodding rapidly, is halfway down the hall by now. The
Administrator shakes his head in disgust and walks past.
The HUGE CART. Which now blocks the door on Eugene's room.

EXT. PHELPS MEMORIAL HOSPITAL - CONTINUOUS
Kimberly seems to have ditched the cops. She speeds the pick up through the medical
facility.

EXT. EMERGENCY ROOM - DAY
The pick up skids to a halt in front of the hospital. Kimberly,
Thomas and Clear run outside and into the building.

INT. PRIVATE ROOM - DAY
The OXYGEN HOSE hisses, but is drowned out by the volume of the TV.
Eugene's eyes dart frantically as a blaring fast food commercial ends. The n, a NEWS
REPORT comes on. The BANNER:

ROUTE 18 TRAGEDY
Footage showing grieving families, wreaths on doors, yellow ribbons, and emergency
crews pulling wreckage apart, dissolve together over:

ANCHOR WOMAN (O.S.)
Mor e tears were shed this morning in the wake of yesterday's tragedy that rocked the
Tri -State area...
Suddenly, the FRAYED ELECTRIC CORD of Eugene's TV begins sparking.
The sound DROPS OUT, the picture SPUTTERS.
Eugene goes white with terror. He looks back to
The broken OXYGEN TUBE. HISSING softly. The BEEPS of the EEG machine
frantically increase. Eugene reaches for the nurse call switch.
Mockingly out of reach by mere millimeters.

INT. NURSES STATION - DAY
Clear, Kimberly and Thomas dash toward the main desk.

CLEAR
Isabella Cruz. What room's she in?

RECEPTIONIST
I'm sorry, I can't give out that info unless you're a relative.

CLEAR
I'm her sister.
The Receptionist eyes her dubiously.

RECEPTIONIST

I'll have to see your ID, Ms. Cruz.

Clear vaults over the counter, straight-arms the Receptionist and seizes the computer. Thomas and Kimberly look on, stunned.

CLEAR

Delivery rooms are downstairs.

I'll find Eugene and catch up with you.

Kimberly and Thomas hurry to the elevator banks...then reconsider and enter the stairwell.

INT. PRIVATE ROOM - CONTINUOUS

Eugene scratches the top sheet of the bed, trying to inch the call- switch closer and closer to him. But it won't budge.

A RAT APPEARS behind Eugene's pillow, CRAWLS over his chest and disappears by his stomach!

He pounds desperately on the empty food tray, his side rails, looks toward the door

INT. HOSPITAL CORRIDOR - CONTINUOUS

Outside the door, you can't hear a thing in the bustling hallway as people rush by. Kimberly and Thomas rush past his door, lost.

THOMAS

Hurry, I think she's this way.

BACK TO EUGENE

His eyes scream insanely, but he respirator tube prevents any sound from escaping him. And that's when the RAT appears on the floor and begins gnawing on the respirator's power cord!

When Eugene sees this, the EEG machine climbs off the charts.

INT. NURSES STATION - CONTINUOUS

Clear takes off down the hallway. The Receptionist, shaken, dials her phone.

RECEPTIONIST

Security?

INT. DELIVERY ROOM - CONTINUOUS

The Obstetrician voices concern.

OBSTETRICIAN

Listen to me, Isabella, I need you to stop pushing.

ISABELLA

What's wrong? IS the baby all right?

OBSTETRICIAN

It's a breach. If I can't reverse it, we may need to do a Caesarian.
The Obstetrician's hands go to work. Steve looks ill.

STEVE
Maybe I should step outside.

INTERCUT KIMBERLY AND THOMAS
Running down the corridor.

PA ANNOUNCEMENT
Code Blue in Delivery Room 6. Code
Blue!

INT. PRIVATE ROOM - DAY
The rat GNAWS away at Eugene's power cord, Eugene looks trapped, helpless, tortured.
His eyes dart from the sparking TV to the gnawed power cord to the useless call- switch.

INT. HOSPITAL CORRIDOR - CONTINUOUS
Clear walks up and down the corridor, scanning room numbers as she passes. A -169, A- 171, A-173...

CLEAR
B-187...B-187...
A HAND suddenly GRABS Clear and shoves her against the wall. REVEAL A SECURITY GUARD leering at her.

SECURITY GUARD
Just where do you think you're going?
Clear struggles to get away, getting sympathetic looks from an OLD
MAN walking a rolling IV STAND down the corridor.

INT. DELIVERY ROOM - CONTINUOUS
Isabella is pushing again.

OBSTETRICIAN
Almost there. I see the head...
The NURSE takes a pair of SCISSORS off a tray.

INT. HOSPITAL CORRIDOR - CONTINUOUS
Clear plays possum, offering no resistance to the Security Guard as the Old Man wheels his IV STAND along.
Suddenly, Clear grabs the stand - and WHAMS the heavy wheeled base into the Guard's BALLS! As the Guard recoils, she thoughtfully hands the IV back to the Old Man and runs.

INT. DELIVERY ROOM 0 CON
The Nurse is startled when Kimberly and Thomas BURST THROUGH the door. In the BG, a puzzled Steve peeks inside until Kimberly pulls the door closed.

NURSE
What are you doing in here? Get the hell out! Right now!
Finally we hear the BABY CRY! The Nurse immediately moves in to swaddle the newborn. Dr. Kalarjian beams at the very groggy looking
Isabella.

OBSTETRICIAN
Isabella, look down and see your son.
To the confusion of everyone around them, Kimberly and Thomas BURST
INTO CHEERS! They jump, dance and hug each other.
It's a magical moment

EXT. EUGENE'S PRIVATE ROOM - CONTINUOUS
The RAT stops gnawing. The TV stops sparking. A wave of intense relief washes over Eugene. He pantomimes reaching into his shirt pocket and lighting a victory cigar.

INT. HOSPITAL CORRIDOR - CONTINUOUS
Relaxed and invigorated, Kimberly and Thomas giddily exit the delivery room as Clear runs up to them.

CLEAR
A guard grabbed me before I could find Eugene.

THOMAS
Don't sweat it. It's over.

CLEAR
She had the baby?

KIMBERLY
New life defeats death. We've done it. Death has to rewrite the list.
We're safe.
Steve watches, confused, as Clear whoops with delight and HUGS the others.
Clear laughs with a relief that seems completely foreign to her.
Kimberly laughs with her, then is suddenly rocked by a vision

HARD CUT TO:
UNKOWN POV
Looking up a the EEG machine. Flatlined!

THOMAS (O.S.)
Kimberly! Are you okay?!

INT. HOSPITAL CORRIDOR - BACK TO PRESENT
Kimberly, on the ground, looks frazzled as she SNAPS out of her trance. Thomas helps her to her feet.

THOMAS
Are you okay? You just face planted!

KIMBERLY
I know how it feels to be dead.
Her lips blue, Kimberly shivers uncontrollably. Clear sees TWO
SECURITY GUARDS round a distant corner and quickly walks the others toward an
EMERGENCY LOADING ZONE.

CLEAR
What did you see?

KIMBERLY
I was dead. And came back to life.
An EEG machine. Where's Eugene?

THOMAS
But it's over. Isabella's baby was the key. You saw her die and everything, right?

KIMBERLY
I don't...what if I made a mistake?

THOMAS
Impossible. She was on the onramp.
Kimberly reluctantly closes her eyes and remembers.

CUT TO:
PREVIOUSLY UNSEEN
Moment of the pile-up premonition. A WHITE VAN in fr ont of Kimberly suddenly slams on its brakes and pulls onto the shoulder.
Kimberly screams, swerving around the van just in time to avoid an accident.

BACK TO:
Kimberly, overcome with self- doubt.

KIMBERLY
I'm not sure... I don't think
Isabella was ever destined to die in the pile -up.

THOMAS
Then what's the premonition of the lake supposed to mean?

CLEAR
Can you remember anything about it?
Kimberly shuts her eyes, remembering:

EXT. LAKE - DAY
POV DRIVER
Grease-covered hands reach out toward a steering wheel of a white van speeding out of control TOWARD A LAKE!
The van crashes through a railing and PLUNGES into the water. In moments, the van fills with water, the driver inside trapped.
Drowning. Horrible.
And on the rearview mirror, six floral scented AIR-FRESHNERS.

BACK TO:
Kimberly looks down at her grease -covered hands and looks ill.

KIMBERLY
...the Same hands from the van.
Finally everything makes sense to Clear.

CLEAR
It's you Kimberly. The premonitions are about you.
Kimberly trembles, refusing to accept what she's hearing.

KIMBERLY
No! It can't be.

CLEAR
(suddenly remembering)
I have to save Eugene!
Clear leaves Kimberly and Thomas together. Kimberly verges on tears and Thomas consoles her with a hug.

IN THE BACKGROUND
Clear looks at passing room numbers while hurrying down the corridor.
She comes to a room with a HUGE CART parked outside, blocking the door. She looks up to see - B -187.
Clear leans into it, pushing it out of the way of the door.

CLEAR
Eugene? Are you in there?

EUGENE'S ROOM
Eugene strains to hear through the thick door.

CLEAR (O.S.)
Can you hear me? I'm coming in .
An intense wave of relief washes over Eugene.

BACK TO:
As Kimberly hugs Thomas, she watches Clear push the cart past the door.

ORDERLY (O.S.)
Make way, make way lovebirds.
Kimberly spins as Eugene's Orderly passes her; a paper, pen and a crossword book in one hand, A BIRTHDAY CAKE in the other.
The CAKE reads "Happy Birthday Gregory". The THIRTEEN SPARKLING CANDLES on top ODDLY FRAME Clear's head.

KIMBERLY
Oh no...
The Orderly speeds down the corridor toward Clear, whose hand reaches for Eugene's door handle. She leans into it

ORDERLY
(to Clear)
Thanks hon, the Henzels are going crazy for this thing.

THOMAS AND KIMBERLY
Watch as Clear opens the door, briefly revealing Eugene, a whoosh of
Oxygen

BOOM!!!
Clear's body is obscenely hurled END OVER END towards the CAMERA, heading straight for Kimberly and Thomas!
Thomas throws himself and Kimberly around the corner to prevent being crushed by Clear's lifeless body!
The hospital erupts in total chaos. Just as Kimberly is about to break down completely, she sees
A WOMAN hurrying down the hallway in their direction, pushing a crash cart.
Kimberly sees the nametag: KALARJIAN.

KIMBERLY
Nurse Kalarjian...

DR. KALARJIAN
Doctor Kalarjian. Excuse me, please.

ANGLE ON CART
DEFRIBULATOR PADDLES rest on top. And then Dr. Kalarjian passes them toward the area of the explosion.

KIMBERLY OMINOUSLY TURNS, the camera following her view, until she sees a small lake across the street from the hospital.

KIMBERLY
Oh my God. That's it. The lake.
The EEG machine. Nurse Kalarjian.

THOMAS
What?
Just then, an AMBULANCE SKIDS up to the nearest entrance. PARAMEDICS jump out and run towards the blast site.

KIMBERLY
You can't cheat destiny. I know what I have to do to save us. I have to die.

THOMAS
That's crazy. You can't give up now. We can still fight this thing.
But Kimberly isn't listening. She stares through the glass doors at the

AMBULANCE
A red stripe down the side, but the hood is completely white. Six floral scented air-fresheners hang from the rearview. The 'van' from her vision! And it's running!

KIMBERLY
I have to do this.
Kimberly wipes tears from her eyes, kisses Thomas' cheek, then turns and runs before he can speak.

EXT. HOSPITAL ENTRANCE - CONTINUOUS
Kimberly heads right for the open ambulance. The driver's door almost seems to swing open for her as she gets in.

INT. HOSPITAL ENTRANCE - CONTINUOUS
Thomas frantically tries to get through the electric doors, which
SPARK and short out. He struggles to pry them apart.

EXT. HOSPITAL ENTRANCE - CONTINUOUS
Kimberly shifts into gear and speeds off. Thomas squeezes through the doors and runs after her. An EMT, the driver of the stolen ambulance, rushes outside.

EMT
What the fuck?!

EXT. LAKE - DAY
Thomas chases the ambulance, watching helplessly as it barrels over curbs, pylons and a fence, ultimately plunging straight into the lake!

Thomas sprints to the lake as fast as he can - the EMT trailing far behind.

INSIDE THE AMBULANCE
Kimberly panics as the ambulance fills with water and she takes a final gasp of air

ON THE LAKE'S EDGE
Thomas stares in horror at the percolating air bubbles as the vehicle descends below the surface and he dives in!

UNDERWATER
Thomas swims into the dark, murky water. Deeper and deeper, he g ets to the ambulance and tries to open the door. Stuck. He withdraws his baton and BANGS on the glass - nothing!
He tries coming up for air, but his pants snag on the jagged metal of the twisted bumper. He squirms frantically...
And as his exhausted body loses consciousness, everything

FADE TO BLACK.
INT. HOSPITAL ROOM - DAY
BLACKNESS.
DR. KALARJIAN (O.S.)
Ready and...CLEAR!
The SHOCK of defribulator paddles brings Kimberly back to life.

KIMBERLY'S POV
Looking up at Dr. Kalarjian, all she can see is part of a woman's face and a partial nametage reading "Kalarjian".
It would appear as if she's choking Kimberly, but
An EEG MONITOR turns from a flatline to a steady heartbeat, the same
POV as the premonition.

NURSE
She's back!

DR. KALARJIAN
Five CC's of narcodon. I want her stabilized and prepped for ICU.
Kimberly turns her head to see

THOMAS
Unconscious, CPR being performed on him by the EMT (who's now soaking wet). Thomas doesn't respond.
An INTERN opens an eyelid, points a flashlight at his eyes. Shakes his head, nothing.
The sopping wet EMT goes back to performing CPR.
Finally, Thomas coughs up water, chokes, gasps for air, then BOLTS

UPRIGHT.

THOMAS
Kimberly?!
He turns to see Kimberly reaching out for him. Immeasurably relieved, he takes her hand and allows himself to be eased back down to the platform. Kimberly's eyes fill with tears.

KIMBERLY
(whispering)
Welcome back. We did it. For real.

THOMAS
I know. I can feel it too.
Outside, a parting of dark clouds causes a shaft of sunlight to flood into the hospital. Its light covers Kimberly and Thomas with an ethereal glow. There are no more doubts; they've won.
They exchange meek, yet triumphant smiles in the smoky, chaotic hospital.

SLOW DISSOLVE TO:
EXT. PARK - DAY
We are at a summer barbecue. Frisbee, lawn darts, croquet, et.
Everyone's happy.

TITLE CARD: FIVE MONTHS LATER
ANGLE ON
Shish -Kabob entering a mouth.

REVEAL
Kimberly taking a bite, relishing the taste and calmly pulling the metal skewer from her mouth.

KIMBERLY
My God, this is delicious. I can't believe I used to be a vegan.
Thomas, out of uniform, takes a bite of his own. As the metal skewer is deep in his mouth
A running FRISBEE PLAYER accidentally bumps into Thomas! But no harm.
Thomas gives the guy a friendly pat and goes back to rewrapping his mouth around the shish-kabob.

MR. BURROUGHS (O.S.)
So what's the deal, Thomas? Three months and you still haven't asked my daughter out on a date.
Kimberly turns red as Mr. Burroughs appears and takes a seat.

THOMAS
What's wrong with a platonic relationship?

MR. GIBBONS
Platonic my ass. That's for ugly women.

KIMBERLY
For God's sake, leave him alone,
Dad.

THOMAS
(smiling)
Yeah, don't make me cite you for harassment.

MR. GIBBONS
Oh please. I'm not hurting anyone.
(looking around, lowering voice)
Besides, if you can beat Death, what's he got to worry about me for?
Mr. Gibbons sits down at the table with two plates of food. His wife,
MRS. GIBBONS, joins.

MR. GIBBONS
You know, you still never explained to us how you did it.
It seems by now everyone's familiar with the concept.

THOMAS
Well, technically when we died, we gave Death what it wanted. And by the time we were revived, it had already moved on to graver pastures.
Mrs. Gibbons makes a face, finding the discourse distasteful. She changes the conversation.

MRS. GIBBONS
You know, I'm having the greatest day?

KIMBERLY
Food's great too, Mrs. Gibbons.
Big props to you and Brian.

MRS. GIBBONS
Our...pleasure. So, ready for the back-to -school season? NYU, right?

KIMBERLY
Three short glorious weeks away.

MRS. GIBBONS
Sounds wonderful. I wish I were going myself.

MR. GIBBONS
(to Mr. Burroughs)

You may want to think twice about letting her live in the village,
Bob. Our eldest daughter moved there and came back with piercings all over her face.
(looks grave)
Among other places.
A chorus of friendly laughter.

BRIAN (O.S.)
Dad used to call her the pincushion. From Hellraiser.
BRIAN enters frame, soaking up fresh laughter. He holds a plate full of raw chicken
fillets and some long, wooden matches.

BRIAN
Dad, you had the spatula last, right?

MR. GIBBONS
Sure, here.
Mr. Gibbons hands it over and Brian saunters away from camera,
SLIGHTLY OUT OF FOCUS, toward the barbecue, his body framed between
Kimberly and Thomas' heads.

KIMBERLY
Brian looks like he's having fun.

MR. GIBBONS
Sure does. Owes it to that friend of yours, in a way.
Mr. Gibbons immediately regrets having said that.

KIMBERLY
How's that?

MR. GIBBONS
Well, Brian was nearly hit by an ambulance the day...but your friend
Rory pulled him back at the last second.
Kimberly and Thomas ominously turn their heads around. In the BG,
Brian fidgets in front of the barbecue.

MRS. GIBBONS
You never told me that, Peter.
Boy, that was lucky.
BOOM!!! The PROPANE TANK blows Brian to smithereens. A deafening silence
follows, punctuated when Brian's ARM lands on Mrs. Gibbons' plate. PLOP.

FADE TO BLACK.